THE
ALLERGY COOKBOOK

Delicious recipes for every day and special occasions

CAROL G. EMERLING
and
EUGENE O. JONCKERS

Foreword by JOSEPH F. KELLEY, M.D.

BARNES & NOBLE BOOKS

A DIVISION OF HARPER & ROW, PUBLISHERS

New York, Evanston, San Francisco, London

the text of this book is printed on 100% recycled paper

A hardcover edition of this book was published by Doubleday and Co., Inc. It is here reprinted by arrangement.

FOREWORD

Some people do have allergic reactions to certain foods. This is fact. Symptoms that may be caused by these reactions are inflammation of the eyes, ears, nose, or throat or wheezing, cough, hives, localized or generalized swelling of the body, itching of the skin, and skin rashes such as infantile eczema. Less frequently, food sensitivity may manifest itself as migraine-type headache, large or small bowel irritability, and in extreme cases an allergic shock that may cause death.

When there is suspicion of food allergy, the offender must be identified. Study of dietary patterns, sometimes skin testing and a variety of food elimination diets are used to uncover these culprits. Foods causing rapid and violent reactions are usually easily identified. Those causing constant or frequently recurring but less severe problems are more difficult to discover.

Since chronic, constantly present symptoms are often caused by foodstuffs that are encountered daily, the task of eliminating these from the usual diet may become a seemingly unsolvable problem, especially for those who must cook not only for the allergic individual, but also for a family.

Housewives have become so dependent upon prepared, prepackaged, and precooked foods that they are terrified at the thought of having to "cook from scratch." There are many young women who have never cooked any fresh vegetable except perhaps a potato, nor made a cake or pastry other than from a commercial mix.

To eliminate a food from a diet successfully, one must first adopt an attitude of adventurous eating, realizing that he may become familiar with foods and recipes that he might otherwise never have encountered. To ease things for the cook and to help keep the suspected allergic person from feeling left out, it is wise for the entire family to eat the same foods; make the same eliminations and enjoy the same new gastronomical experiences. It is particularly important for the allergic child not to be made to feel different from others in the family or deprived because of illness. He must be made to understand that keeping him from eating a certain food is not punishment but something that will keep him physically well. He must also have available a reasonable substitute for the forbidden food.

When Mrs. Emerling first learned of the food restrictions needed for her children, I am certain she too felt desperate. How could a practicing attorney run a household and feed a family without "convenience" foods? Being accustomed to doing extensive research in her profession, she went about the food elimination task in the same way. She discovered that there are many satisfactory ingredient substitutes for groups of foods that must be eliminated entirely. She began researching, experimenting, and consulting with friends, among them an expert chef, Mr. Eugene O. Jonckers. The job proved to be long but fruitful. Mrs. Emerling and Mr. Jonckers clearly demonstrate that one who has food allergy can be a true epicure.

JOSEPH F. KELLEY, M.D.

CONTENTS

Recipes for ingredients marked with an asterisk (*) may be located by consulting the Index.

INTRODUCTION

So you have food allergies! Well, before you start feeling too special, let us tell you that approximately fifty per cent of the people in the United States have the same problem. That fifty per cent figure is a conservative estimate, based on careful surveys. A sporting guess would rate the percentage considerably higher.

The majority of people with allergies are those who get hives or a similar reaction from a small number of foods; and it can be any food—allergies are not confined to specific foods; one can be sensitive to *anything*. In addition to the normally allergic group, about ten percent of the population suffer from severe allergy and seek professional help.

Allergies may appear as early as the first few months of life. Allergy to milk is often the first one, with an increase in the number of food allergies accompanying the increase in the variety of foods children eat as they grow. But allergic sensitivities can develop at any subsequent time during one's life. Very often they become apparent during times of stress.

But, whether you are a member of the over forty per cent of the population who have easily identifiable allergies that can be controlled by diet-watching, or of the ten per cent whose allergies are severe enough to need professional treatment, the food you eat is one of the most important keys to your physical and emotional well-being. The physical aspect is obvious, but one must be allergic to realize the psychological effect of feeling below par over a long period of time.

If you have just discovered a food allergy in your family, you probably registered only moderate concern. It wasn't until your first sortie into label-reading at the local supermarket that the impact of allergic eating made itself felt. It must have seemed that you were allergic to something in practically every blasted can! You were sure that you would either starve to death (slowly, of course) or that food would become a matter of necessity rather than pleasure. (You might even look into existing on vitamin pills or intravenous injections of some sort!)

But, happily, survival lies in following another course. You can *cook!* Webster's dictionary defines the word "cook" as follows:

> "1. To prepare (food) by boiling, roasting, baking, etc. 2. To subject to the action of heat or fire, . . . 3. *Colloq*. To concoct; hence, to tamper with; doctor; . . ."

When we have this definition firmly in mind, we realize that "to prepare" and "to concoct" must be further clarified in terms of what foods to "prepare" and "concoct" with.

Being on an allergy diet means that you must omit the allergy-producing foods from your diet. There are two propositions contained in this statement.

1. You must know what ingredients go into the foods you eat.
2. You must know how to prepare what you want to eat without using "verboten" items.

Thus, the *"raison d'être"* of this book—after assuring you that food can continue to be a diversion as well as a necessity, we present to you the means for accomplishing this feat.

First, it is important to understand that cooking in conformity with allergic needs does not necessarily mean that unusual ingredients must be used. If you do not eat what you are allergic to, are you compelled to eat some strange concoction in its place? Of course not! If you are allergic to chicken, you can still eat beef, veal, lamb, and pork. If you are allergic to cottonseed oil, you can prepare your salad dressings with corn oil, soybean oil, or olive oil. If you are allergic to wheat, you can use arrowroot or barley flour, oats, or cornstarch for baking or as thickening agents in gravies and stews. You can use tapioca or cornstarch in pies. And you can prepare breads with rye flour as well as with other non-wheat flours.

You do, however, get a bit far-out when you proceed to make a delectable chocolate cake without using any chocolate; or no-chocolate chocolate brownies! You use carob powder in these items, and then dare anyone to tell you it isn't really chocolate!

In this book we have tried to present a variety of good recipes to help you in choosing what you want to eat from the list of what you are permitted to eat. Some allergy dieters will not need to go beyond merely selecting interesting recipes having perfectly "normal" ingredients.

Those who are allergic to various food additives and preservatives can prepare anything they like in their kitchens—their criterion would be that the food is home-prepared, rather than commercially prepared.

Those who are allergic to foods which are usually eaten alone, rather than in combination with other foods, need to choose substitutes for their allergic foods. For example, we have prepared a list of fruit and vegetable juices. If orange juice is not permitted, you can have apple, cherry, cranberry, etc., etc.

The soup chapter contains a list of flours that can be used in making roux for soups. This list contains the tablespoon equivalents for one ounce of each of the flours, since the flour requirement of each recipe is given in ounces. Thus, any of the thick soups can be made with any one of nine different flours. Just choose the one to which you are not allergic.

While appetizers, salads, vegetables, meat, fish, cheese, and eggs are largely a matter of selecting the recipe with the permitted ingredients, the baked goods and breads go into unusual, sometimes even exotic, combinations and ingredients. Potato starch cakes, rice flour cookies, barley flour bread, and carob powder chocolates are offered along with the more normal (but still delicious) recipes for meringue cookies and ground nut tortes.

From the list of oils in Chapter One, you can select a permissible one and proceed immediately with the preparation of a gourmet salad dressing. You can select an appropriate flour and make an elegant sauce.

If you are allergic to milk, you can make your own synthetic ice cream. If it's corn you can't eat (corn syrup is used as a sweetener in all commercial foods), you can make your own candies and syrups for soft drinks.

The Appendix at the end of the book contains several Indexes to aid you in finding the recipes suited to your needs. For example, there is an Egg-free Index, a Milk-and-wheat-free Index, and so on. After looking through these Indexes you can pinpoint the ones that will be most helpful to you.

We have given here but a brief sampling of the uses of this book in feeding the allergic person. It has been prepared to give you ideas as well as recipes, and to show you that you can enjoy eating while adhering strictly to doctor's orders.

CAROL G. EMERLING
EUGENE O. JONCKERS

CHAPTER 1

ALLERGY COOKING GUIDE

On the whole, this book is laid out like an ordinary cookbook. You can use it just as you would any other cookbook, picking out those recipes you would like to serve your family or guests.

Or, you can use it to solve your allergy cooking problems. The book is geared to helping you make easy adjustments and substitutions for a restricted diet. In this chapter you will find lists of common food allergies and many common food products containing the forbidden item. It also has a list of many common alcoholic beverages and what they contain, a list of herbs and spices, what they are made from and where to use them, and lists of cheeses, fats, oils, flours, starches, and fruits and vegetable juices, so as to acquaint you with various alternatives to the foods you have come to rely on.

Further, at the beginning of each chapter is an Allergy Key, which will alert you to the most common allergies dealt with in the chapter. But, since allergies are slippery things, and people can become allergic to anything on God's green earth, the task of marking every possible food sensitivity was an impossible one for the authors. You will have to do your own selecting from the recipes set forth, and sometimes even your own substituting. But always remember, the result is worth the effort!

COMMON FOOD ALLERGENS—
SOME FOODS THEY MAY BE FOUND IN

Below are suggestions of possible forms a food may take. This is not meant to be an all inclusive list. It is important that you read the labels of all foods to determine their contents.

CORN

Whole corn in its various forms, breakfast cereals, cornmeal, corn oil, corn sugar (used in commercial products such as candy, ice cream, jellies), cornstarch, corn syrup, corn whiskeys (Bourbon), margarine. Some baking powders contain cornstarch. Confectioners' sugar contains cornstarch.

COTTONSEED

Candies, especially chocolate, cottonseed oil, many fried foods, mayonnaise, margarine, salad oil, shortening.

EGG

Eggs in their various cooked forms, custards, most baked goods, many ice creams and ices, noodles and spaghetti, many salad dressings. Eggs are often used as a binder in foods like hamburgers and meat loaf.

MILK

Milk, candies, cream, cheeses, ice cream, margarine, many baked goods, many sauces, often used as a filler in sausages, hamburger, and similar products. Non-fat milk solids are used in the preparation of many commercial food products.

SOY BEAN

Soy bean flour, ice cream, soy sauce, steak sauce, mayonnaise, margarine, salad dressings, shortening; lecithin is usually derived from soy flour and is used in many commercial food products; sausage products may contain soy fillers.

WHEAT

Alcoholic beverages, breads, baked goods, breakfast cereals, breading, candies, flour, macaroni, malt, noodles, spaghetti. Wheat starch is used in many commercial foods such as soups and as a thickening agent in sauces and dressings. Many sausage products use wheat as a filler and binder.

ALCOHOLIC BEVERAGES

BEER AND ALE: Beverage made by fermentation of crushed cereal. Ingredients are yeast, hops, and barley malt. A few German beers are made from a wheat malt instead of the barley malt. There is now no difference between ingredients in beer and ale. However, black beers (Stout and Porter) are never called "ale."

BRANDY: Most are made by distilling fermented grape juice. A few are distilled from other fruit juices; for example, applejack and Calvados are distilled from apples; Kirsch and Schwartzwalder are made from cherries.

GIN: English and American gin are distilled from barley, rye, and either corn or maize, with juniper berries, coriander seeds, angelica root, and other ingredients as flavorings. Dutch gin is distilled from barley and rye and is flavored with juniper berries and other flavorings. Sloe gin is made from sloe berries steeped in dry gin.

LIQUEURS AND CORDIALS: Liqueurs are made from relatively strong alcohol that is as pure and neutral as possible; then sugar or syrup and various flavorings are added.

Cordials are made by the infusion process in which alcohol and sugar are added to various fresh fruit juices. Flavoring agents frequently used are aniseed, coriander, fennel, wormwood, gentian, sassafras, amber, hyssop, mint, thyme, angelica, citron, lemon peel, orange peel, peppermint, cinnamon, cloves, iris, caraway, tea, coffee, and cassia.

SOME INGREDIENTS IN WELL-KNOWN LIQUEURS: *Absinthe*—wormwood and anise; *Anisette*—aniseed; *Aquavit*—caraway seed; *Benedictine*—brandy; *Chartreuse*—brandy; *Cointreau*—orange peel; *Crème de Cacao*—cocoa; *Crème de Menthe*—mint; *Curaçao*—orange peel and rum; *Drambuie*—Scotch whiskey; *Grand Marnier*—orange peel and brandy; *Kirsch*—the morello cherry; *Kümmel*—caraway seeds; *Maraschino*—the marasca cherry; *Triple Sec*—orange peel.

RUM: Distilled from sugarcane.

TEQUILA: Distilled from mezcal, a small cactus plant.

VODKA: Usually distilled from rye and potatoes; sometimes barley is used instead of rye.

WHISKIES: *American*—Bourbon or corn whiskey—made with barley or rye malt. Malt whiskey—made predominantly with barley. Rye whiskey—made predominantly with rye; may use either a rye or barley malt. Wheat whiskey—made predominantly with wheat; may also use a barley or rye malt. *Irish Whiskey*—Pot-still whiskeys usually are made from barley, oats, wheat, and rye; the patent still whiskeys are made from maize, barley, rye, and oats. *Scotch Whiskey*—Pot-still whiskies are made from barley and are usually stored in sherry casks; patent still whiskies are made from maize, barley, rye, and oats. The smoky Scotches result when the grain is dried over a peat fire.

WINES: Wines are made from fermented grape juice. Fortified wines (i.e., sherry, port, Madeira, vermouth) have brandy distilled from wine added to increase the alcoholic strength. Sake is a Japanese wine made from rice.

CHEESES

Below is a list of some cheeses and what they are made from. This will be of particular interest to those with allergies to cow's milk. This is not meant to be an exhaustive survey, but only a sampling of suggestions.

COW'S MILK CHEESES: American, Bel Paese, Bleu, Brie, Camembert, Carre de l'Est, Cheddar, Cottage, Coulommiers, Cream, Edam, Gorganzola, Gouda, Gruyère, Liederkranz, Limburger, Muenster, Neufchatel, Parmesan, Pont l'Eveque, Port du Salut, Provolone, Reblochon, Ricotta, Romano, St. Paulin, Swiss, Tomme au Marc.

EWE'S (SHEEP) MILK CHEESE: Genuine Roquefort.

GOAT'S MILK CHEESES: Banon, Cabecou, Chabichou, St. Marcellin. Any French cheese with *chèvre* on the label is a goat cheese.

FLOURS AND STARCHES

FOR USE IN BAKING:

Carob powder—Made from ground pod of the tamarind tree; used as a chocolate substitute, it imparts a chocolate flavor and color.

Barley—Particularly good for cakes but can be used in almost all baked goods; its products retain moistness for several days.

Cornmeal—Imparts a coarse texture but is very tasty in various breads.

Cornstarch—Do not use the waxy type for baking; light in texture; must be handled carefully or it will lump.

Ground nuts—Used in tortes, cookies, and other baked goods.

Oatmeal and rolled oats—Usually used in combination with other flours in cookies and breads.

Potato starch—Imparts a light, fluffy texture; used alone in some cakes and in combination with other flours in breads and rolls.

Rice—Do not use waxy type for baking; a very light flour, it is usually combined with other flours.

Rye—Can be used as a wheat substitute in most things but it produces a much heavier-textured product.

Soybean—Should be used only in combination with other flours; its texture is somewhat oily.

Wheat—The standard baking flour.

THICKENING AGENTS OTHER THAN WHEAT

Arrowroot—Use 1 tablespoon arrowroot for 2½ tablespoons wheat flour.

Barley flour—Use in same proportions as wheat flour.

Cornstarch—Use waxy type; use one-half the wheat quantity.

Oatmeal—Use in same proportions as wheat flour.

Potato starch—Use one-half the wheat quantity.

Rice flour—Use the waxy type; use one-half the wheat quantity.

Sago—Use one-half the wheat quantity.

Tapioca—Use one-half the wheat quantity.

FRUIT AND VEGETABLE JUICES

Apple, Apricot, Carrot, Cherry, Cranberry, Fig, Grape, Grapefruit, Lemon, Lime, Orange, Papaya, Peach, Pear, Pineapple, Prune, Raspberry, Sauerkraut, Strawberry, and Tomato.

SALT

So far as is known, plain table salt (sodium chloride) will not create an allergy problem. However, you should read the label on the salt box to make sure it does not contain an additive or filler (such as cornstarch) to which you might be allergic.

PEPPER

Usually, if you are allergic to pepper you will be allergic to both black and white pepper. As pepper substitutes we would suggest using ginger or dry mustard in the same quantity as pepper or cayenne pepper in one-half the quantity.

HERBS AND SPICES

Herbs and spices should be used sparingly and not too many in combination, or one flavor kills the other. Seasonings are used to enhance the flavor of food, not to drown it out.

Herb—A seed-producing plant with soft or succulent tissue.

Spice—An aromatic vegetable used to season food.

Allspice—Made from the dried reddish-brown berry of the pimento or allspice tree of the myrtle family native to the West Indies and Central America; also called pimento and Jamaica pepper; has the combined flavor of cinnamon, clove, nutmeg, and juniper berry; used for sauces and dressings.

Angelica—The herb *angelica* in the carrot family; it has a slight licorice flavor; used for fruit cakes and decorating; usually comes in candied form.

Anise—The herb *pimpinella anisum* in the carrot family; it has a slight licorice flavor; used for breads and for seasoning some vegetables and in special recipes to replace absinthe.

Basil—Leaf of *Ocimum basilicum* in the mint family; used for dressings and vegetables.

Bay leaf—Leaf of the sweet bay tree, *Laurus nobilis,* of the laurel family. Use with veal, chicken, pork, and soups.

Capers—Flower buds and young berries of the caper plant; used in sauces and dressings and as a garnish.

Caraway seed—The seeds from an aromatic plant in the carrot family; used in breads, salads, and vegetables.

Cardamom—Seeds of the aromatic East Indian plant *Elettaria cardamomum;* use as you would cinnamon or cloves; used in baked goods and sauces.

Cassia buds—Immature fruits of the tree *Cinnamomum Cassia;* used in breads and pickles.

Cayenne—Made from the powdered ripe dried fruit of *Capsicum;* used in sauces, dressings, meats, salads, soups, and vegetables.

Celery seeds—The dried seed-like fruits of a wild celery; used in salads, dressings, meats, and fish.

Chervil—Leaves of an aromatic plant of the carrot family; used in fish, meats, salads, dressings, sauces, vegetables, and as a garnish.

Chives—Leaves of a plant of the onion family; can be used anywhere onion can be used.

Cinnamon—Made from the bark of the cassia tree; used on fruits, custards, puddings, in breads and baked goods.

Clove—The dried flower bud of a tropical tree, *Eugenia aromatica,* of the myrtle family; used on fruits, meats, sauces, and vegetables.

Coriander—Fruit of the coriander plant; used in baked goods, dressings, marinades, and soups.

Cumin seed—Seed of the cumin plant; its flavor is similar to caraway; used in meats, curries, cheese dishes, and vegetables.

Curry powder—A condiment consisting of ground spices blended according to the type of food to be curried; commercial curry powder usually contains coriander, fenugreek, turmeric, cumin, pepper, bay leaves, celery seed, nutmeg, cloves, onion, cayenne, orange peel, and ginger; used in sauces for eggs, fish, meats, and vegetables.

Dill—A plant of the carrot family; both the seeds and leaves are used; used in cheese, fish, meats, salads, soups, and vegetables.

Fennel—Seed of a plant of the carrot family; used in dressings, salads, soups, and vegetables.

Filé—Sassafras; the dried bark of the root of a tree of the laurel family; used in fish, meats, and sauces.

Garlic—A bulbous herb, *Allium sativum,* of the lily family; used in fish, meats, sauces, and dressings.

Ginger—Made from the dried root of the plant *Zingiber officinale;* used in fruits, vegetables, poultry, and puddings.

Horseradish—Made from the root of the plant *Armoracia rusticana;* used in fish, meats, sauces, and dressings.

Leeks—A leafy variety of onion; used in soups, salads, sauces, and dressings, and wherever onions can be used.

Mace—Made from the dried shell of the nutmeg; used in vegetables and sauces.

Marjoram—A plant of the mint family; used in eggs, fish, meats, salads, sauces and dressings, and vegetables.

Mint—A green leafy aromatic plant; used in fruits, meats, salads, dressings and sauces, vegetables, desserts, and as a garnish.

Mustard—The ground seed of the *Brassica* family; *Brassica alba* yields white mustard and *Brassica nigra* yields black mustard; used in salads, vegetables, and sauces and dressings.

Nutmeg—The aromatic seed of the tree *Myristica fragrans;* used in fruits and vegetables.

Onion—A bulb of the lily family; used in soups, fish, meats, salads, sauces, dressings, and vegetables.

Oregano—Wild marjoram; used in fish, meats, salads, sauces, and dressings.

Paprika—Ground from the fruit of the bonnet pepper, *Capsicum tetragonum;* used in cheeses, fish, meats, sauces and dressings, also in vegetables, and as a garnish.

Parsley—A small green plant of the carrot family; used in soups, salads, dressings, and as a garnish.

Pepper—From the plant *Piper nigrum;* the dried berries yield black pepper; white pepper is the dried ripe seeds without their coatings; used in fish, meats, salads, sauces, dressings, and vegetables.

Poppy seed—The seed of the poppy, *Papaver phoeas;* used in baking.

Rosemary—A fragrant plant of the mint family; used in eggs, fish, meats, and vegetables.

Saffron—The orange-colored dried stigmas of a species of crocus, *Crocus sativus:* often used as a food coloring; used in breads, fish, and rice.

Sage—A plant of the mint family; used in cheeses, fish, meats, and vegetables.

Savory—A plant of the mint family; used in eggs, fish, meats, salads, and vegetables.

Scallions—A variety of onion; used wherever onion can be used.

Sesame seeds—Seed of the East Indian hairy plant, *Sesamum;* used in salads and baked goods.

Shallots—The leaves of a variety of onion; used wherever onions can be used.

Tarragon—A plant of the thistle family; used in eggs, fish, meats, salads, sauces and dressings, and vegetables.

Thyme—A plant of the mint family; used in eggs, fish, meats, salads, sauces, dressings, and vegetables.

Turmeric—The golden-colored root of *Curcuma longa*, a plant of the ginger family; a small amount can be used as a food coloring in place of saffron; used in eggs, rice, sauces, dressings, pickles.

MILK SUBSTITUTES

There are many milk substitutes on the market today in both liquid and powdered form. When purchasing them, check the labels carefully to make sure that milk products are not contained in them. Once a suitable product is obtained, water can be used to mix it to the desired milk or cream-like consistency for use in cooking. In many recipes, fruit juices can be substituted for milk. Remember that the juices will impart flavor, so select one that will harmonize with what you are cooking.

NATURAL SUGARS

Beet sugar—refined from sugar beets. *Brown sugar*—made from cane sugar and molasses. *Cane sugar*—refined from sugar cane. *Confectioners' sugar*—also called powdered sugar; made from cane sugar and cornstarch. *Corn sugar*—made from corn. *Honey*—made by bees from the nectar of flowers. *Maple sugar*—made from the sap of the sugar maple tree. *Molasses*—the reduced liquor from which raw cane sugar has crystallized. *Palm*—obtained from several varieties of palm trees. *Sorghum*—obtained by clarification and concentration of the juice of the sugar sorghum.

OILS

Coconut, Corn, Cottonseed, Olive, Palm, Peanut, Safflower, and Soybean. Substitute olive oil only with caution because it has a distinctive flavor.

FATS

Butter—made from cow's milk. *Chicken fat*—rendered from chicken fat. *Lard*—rendered from pork fat. *Margarine*—made from various vegetable oils; milk solids are often added; sometimes includes animal fats. *Suet*—clear white fat of beef from around the kidneys.

CHAPTER **2**

APPETIZERS AND HORS D'OEUVRES

Allergy Key: Suggestions for appetizers and hors d'oeuvres can be endless. We decided to present a sampling of ideas to you in this chapter and allow you to select for yourself the ones that contain permissible foods.

COLD APPETIZERS AND HORS D'OEUVRES

MARINATED ARTICHOKE HEARTS

> 2 cups cooked artichoke hearts
> 6 tablespoons oil
> 2 tablespoons vinegar
> 1 tablespoon chopped shallots
> ½ teaspoon salt
> ⅛ bay leaf
> 1 tablespoon coarsely chopped parsley

Combine all the ingredients and refrigerate for 6 hours before serving. *Yield:* approximately 6 servings.

MARINATED MUSHROOMS

Prepare as for Marinated Artichoke Hearts* except use 2 cups of fresh white mushrooms instead of the artichoke hearts. *Yield:* approximately 6 servings.

PARISIAN BEEF

1 pound lean beef, well cooked
1 green pepper, finely sliced
1 medium onion, chopped
1 tablespoon coarsely chopped parsley
⅛ bay leaf
3 tablespoons oil
1 tablespoon vinegar
1 teaspoon salt
1 teaspoon prepared mustard
½ teaspoon freshly ground pepper

Mince the beef and add the remaining ingredients. Refrigerate for 6 hours before serving. *Yield:* approximately 8 servings.

DRIED BEEF ROLLS

1 tablespoon horseradish
4 ounces cream cheese
8 slices (thin) dried beef roll

Soften the cream cheese with the horseradish and spread over the beef slices. Roll the slices and refrigerate for a few hours. When ready to serve, slice the rolls into 1-inch-thick pieces. *Yield:* approximately 4 servings.

CANAPES ON TOAST

4 thin slices bread
Butter, margarine, or cream cheese
6 ounces sardines (alternates: tuna fish, salmon,
caviar, herring, shrimp, crab meat, lobster,
cucumbers, liver paste, smoked turkey, salami,
deviled ham, or 3 ounces smoked oysters,
anchovies)
For decoration: pimento, olive slices, chopped
white and yolk of egg

Toast the bread on one side only. Spread the untoasted side with softened butter, margarine, or cream cheese. Add desired topping and decoration. Cut into bite-size pieces. *Yield:* 4 servings.

DEVILED EGGS

4 hard-cooked eggs
3 tablespoons Mayonnaise*
1 teaspoon prepared mustard
Dash Tabasco
Dash Worcestershire sauce
Salt and pepper
Parsley or pimento

Cut eggs in half lengthwise. Remove egg yolks and rinse egg whites with cold water and place upside down on damp cloth to drain. Soften egg yolks with Mayonnaise and add mustard, Tabasco, Worcestershire, salt and pepper. Whip until smooth and creamy. Replace yolk mixture in the whites. Garnish with parsley or pimento and serve. *Yield:* 4 servings.

STUFFED EGGS

4 hard-cooked eggs—whites only
4 tablespoons finely chopped tuna fish (alternates:
   salmon, shrimp, lobster, sardines, herring, deviled
   ham, or chicken)
2 tablespoons Mayonnaise*
Parsley or pimento

Cut eggs in half lengthwise. Remove egg yolks and rinse egg whites with cold water and place upside down on damp cloth to drain. Soften desired filling with Mayonnaise. Place mixture in egg. Garnish with parsley or pimento and serve. Yield: 4 servings.

CHOPPED CHICKEN LIVERS

8 ounces chicken livers
4 tablespoons butter or margarine
1 medium onion, sliced
Sprig thyme
½ bay leaf
1 teaspoon salt
½ teaspoon freshly ground pepper
3 hard-cooked eggs, finely chopped
1 tablespoon dry sherry

Sauté the chicken livers in the butter or margarine with the onion, thyme, bay leaf, salt, and pepper until the livers are thoroughly cooked. Put the mixture through a meat grinder; add the hard-cooked eggs. Add the sherry, place in a mold or bowl, and refrigerate. Yield: approximately 6 servings.

STUFFED FIGS

4 ounces cream cheese
Salt and pepper
8 fresh figs

Soften cream cheese. Add salt and pepper to taste. Stuff the figs with the cheese. Chill and serve. *Yield:* approximately 4 servings.

CHERRYSTONE CLAMS OR BLUEPOINT OYSTERS

20 cherrystone clams or bluepoint oysters
2 tablespoons lemon juice
⅛ teaspoon freshly ground pepper

Serve the clams or oysters on the half shell seasoned with lemon juice and pepper. *Yield:* 4 servings.

FRESH SHRIMP, LOBSTER, CRAB MEAT, OR PRAWNS

2 cups fresh shrimp, lobster, crab meat, or prawns
Lemon wedges
COCKTAIL SAUCE:
½ cup catsup
1 cup chili sauce
1 tablespoon horseradish
2 tablespoons lemon juice
Dash Tabasco
Dash Worcestershire sauce

Serve the fish chilled, with the sauce either on top or in a separate dish. Use the lemon wedges for garnish. *Yield:* 4 servings.

TUNA FISH, SMOKED SALMON, STURGEON, SARDINES, OR SMOKED OYSTERS

> *2 cups tuna fish, smoked salmon, sturgeon, sardines,*
> *   or smoked oysters*
> *Lettuce*
> *1 lemon, quartered*
> *16 crackers or 16 thin slices buttered rye bread*

Serve the seafood on the lettuce in the center of the plate, with the lemon and crackers or bread arranged around the edges. *Yield:* approximately 8 servings.

HOT APPETIZERS AND HORS D'OEUVRES

CAVIAR AND BLINIS

> BLINIS:
> *½ cake yeast*
> *1½ cups milk*
> *1½ cups flour*
> *4 eggs*
> *Pinch salt*
> *Butter or margarine for cooking*
> *8 ounces caviar*

Blinis: Dissolve yeast in 1 cup of lukewarm milk; add 1 cup of flour and make a smooth paste; let ferment for 1 hour at room temperature. Add remaining ½ cup of flour and ½ cup of milk, 4 eggs, and a pinch of salt and let rest for another hour. Melt butter or margarine in an omelet pan; then add enough batter to make a thin pancake (about 1 tablespoon). Serve hot with the caviar, which should be placed in a silver or china dish surrounded with crushed ice. *Yield:* approximately 30 blinis.

CRAB MEAT IMPERIAL ON TOAST

1 tablespoon chopped shallots
1 tablespoon chopped green pepper
2 tablespoons butter or margarine
4 tablespoons Basic Cream Sauce*
6 ounces crab meat
1 teaspoon salt
1 teaspoon dry mustard
1 tablespoon dry white wine
4 slices white bread, toasted
Parmesan cheese

Preheat broiler. Fry the shallots and green pepper briefly in the butter or margarine; add the Cream Sauce and crab meat and simmer until hot throughout. Season with the salt, dry mustard, and wine. Spread on the toast, sprinkle top with Parmesan cheese. Place under the broiler for a few minutes until browned. Cut into bite-size pieces and serve. *Yield:* 4 servings.

TOASTED CHEESE AND BACON

Butter or margarine
4 slices white bread, toasted
4 slices American cheese
4 slices bacon, fried crisp and crumbled

Preheat broiler. Butter the toast and place a slice of cheese on top. Broil for a few minutes until cheese starts to brown. Remove from oven; sprinkle crumbled bacon on top. Cut into bite-size pieces and serve. *Yield:* approximately 6–8 servings.

TINY HAMBURGERS

4 slices white bread, toasted
½ pound fresh ground beef
4 teaspoons catsup

Preheat broiler. Cut toasted bread into silver-dollar-sized pieces. Place 1 tablespoon of meat and 1 teaspoon of catsup on each piece. Broil until cooked, about 5 minutes. Serve hot. *Yield:* 4 servings.

MUSHROOM CAPS STUFFED WITH SHRIMP OR OYSTERS

4 cups large mushroom caps (at least 1 inch diameter)
Butter or margarine for frying mushrooms
Cooked shrimp or raw oysters (approximately 17)
5 tablespoons butter or margarine seasoned with
   chopped shallots, parsley, and salt and pepper
2 tablespoons bread crumbs

Preheat oven to 450 degrees F. Fry large mushroom caps in butter or margarine until tender. Fill center with cooked shrimp or raw oysters. Top with ½ teaspoon seasoned butter or margarine. Sprinkle with fresh bread crumbs and heat at 450 degrees F. for 10 minutes. *Yield:* approximately 17 pieces.

TOASTED NUTS

1 cup nuts, blanched or unblanched
2 teaspoons oil or melted butter or margarine
Salt or seasoned salt, such as onion salt, garlic salt,
   or celery salt, to taste

Preheat oven to 350 degrees F. Place nuts in greased shallow baking pan. Add oil or melted butter or margarine and toss with the nuts. Bake for 5 minutes, toss nuts, season with salt and bake an additional 10 minutes until nuts are browned. Toss a few times while toasting. Turn out on a paper towel and serve hot or cold. *Yield:* 1 cup.

To blanch nuts: Blanching removes the thin skin around nuts. Pour boiling water over the shelled nuts. Let stand in the water no more than a minute. Drain off water and peel the skins off.

BEEF TENDERLOIN TERIYAKI

1 pound lean beef tenderloin tips (trimmed tenderloin tails)
6 tablespoons soy sauce
4 tablespoons oil
1 clove garlic, finely chopped
1 teaspoon salt
½ teaspoon freshly ground pepper

Cut beef into 1-inch cubes. Combine the remaining ingredients and pour over the meat. Refrigerate overnight.

Preheat broiler. Drain the marinade away and broil the meat for 5–10 minutes, until done. Serve on toothpicks. *Yield:* 4 servings.

CHAPTER **3**

SOUPS

Allergy Key: Soup can be used either to start a meal or as a main course in itself. A hearty soup is a good substitute for potatoes, rice, or starchy vegetables. If there is an allergy to any of the vegetables or seasonings used in the recipes, the food causing allergy can be omitted or substituted for.

In those recipes that call for flour, any of the flours or starches listed right below can be used. The table shows the quantity for 1 ounce, but note that the recipes call for 2 ounces of flour.

Roux—a combination of flour and butter or margarine that is cooked for a few minutes, while being stirred constantly. It is a thickener.

Table of flours for making roux:

1 ounce flour	*Equals*
arrowroot	3 tablespoons
barley	4 tablespoons & 1 teaspoon
cornstarch	3 tablespoons
rolled oats	6 tablespoons
potato starch	3 tablespoons
rice flour	3 tablespoons
rye flour	4 tablespoons & 1½ teaspoons
tapioca	2 tablespoons & 2 teaspoons
wheat flour	3 tablespoons & 2 teaspoons

BASIC SOUP STOCKS

BEEF STOCK

3 pounds beef shank   *1 medium turnip*
4 quarts cold water   *2 parsley roots or sprigs*
3 medium carrots   *½ tablespoon salt*
½ stalk celery

Place meat in large pot and add the cold water. Slowly bring the water to a boil. Skim the scum carefully off the top. Add the vegetables and seasoning. Simmer for about 3 hours, until the meat is tender. Add hot water as the water boils off, in order to maintain the 4-quart volume of the liquid. When cooked, remove from fire and cool for ½ hour. Strain and store the stock in the refrigerator. Can be frozen. *Yield:* approximately 4 quarts.

VEAL, GAME, AND POULTRY STOCKS

Substitute 3 pounds of veal, game or poultry for the beef and proceed as for Beef Stock*, but reduce the cooking time to 2 hours. Can be frozen. *Yield:* approximately 4 quarts.

FISH STOCK

1 large onion, sliced   *½ tablespoon salt*
½ stalk celery   *12 whole peppercorns*
2 parsley roots or sprigs   *1 cup dry white wine*
4 pounds fish trimmings   *4 quarts water*
Juice 1 lemon

Place the vegetables in a heavy stewing pan; place the fish trimmings on top of the vegetables; add lemon juice and seasonings. Cover and simmer for 10 minutes. Add the wine and simmer until the liquid is reduced to one-half its volume. Add the water and simmer for 20 minutes. Cool for ½ hour, strain and refrigerate until needed. Can be frozen. *Yield:* approximately 4 quarts.

HEARTY SOUPS

BEER SOUP

> 4 tablespoons butter or margarine
> 2 ounces flour
> 1 quart beer
> Pinch salt, pepper, sugar, and ground cinnamon

Make roux from butter or margarine and flour. Cook on a slow fire for a few minutes. Add the beer and boil for 15 minutes. Add seasonings. Serve with toasted rye bread. Can be frozen. *Yield:* 6–8 servings.

RUSSIAN BORSCH

> 1 pound boneless beef shank or lean chuck
> 2 leeks
> 1 carrot
> 2 celery stalks
> 1 medium-sized onion
> 1 quart water
> 1 tablespoon salt
> 1 sprig fresh or pinch dried marjoram
> 1 sprig fresh parsley
> Pinch pepper
> Pinch fennel seed
> 8 tablespoons cooked grated beets
> 1 cup sour cream or non-dairy sour cream substitute

Cut the beef in thin strips 1 inch long and parboil for 5 minutes. Set aside. Cut into 1 inch lengths the white of the leeks, the carrot, and celery. Dice the onion. Put vegetables and beef in a pot or casserole. Add water and seasonings. Cook on low fire for about 1 hour, until the meat is tender. Serve hot or cold with the grated beets and sour cream or non-dairy sour cream substitute on the side. Can be frozen. *Yield:* 6–8 servings.

GERMAN BORSCH

Proceed as for Russian Borsch*, but add 1 cup of blanched, drained sauerkraut to the ingredients before cooking.

CHERRY SOUP

1 pound fresh cherries (preferably black cherries)
3 cups water
1 strip lemon rind
1 small cinnamon stick
1 cup port wine
2 tablespoons arrowroot starch, cornstarch, or potato
   starch diluted in 2 tablespoons water
1 tablespoon brown sugar

Stone the cherries; set aside a few for garnish, and crush the stones. Place cherries in the water with lemon rind and cinnamon stick and cook over a medium fire for 10 minutes. In a separate pan place the crushed cherry stones and the wine; bring to a boil, then turn off the fire and let stand for 10 minutes.

Strain the cooked cherries and water through a sieve. Thicken by adding the starch solution. Strain the wine into the cherry mixture. Add brown sugar and the cherries for garnish. Serve either hot or cold, with cinnamon toast. Can be frozen. *Yield:* 6–8 servings.

COLD CHICKEN BOMBAY SOUP

1 celery stalk, diced
1 small onion, diced
1 tablespoon butter or margarine
1 tablespoon curry powder
1 small apple, diced
1 pint Chicken Velouté*
1 pint Chicken Stock*
½ cup cream or non-dairy cream substitute
¼ cup dry white wine

Fry the celery and onion in butter or margarine for a few minutes. Add curry powder and blend well. Add apple, Chicken Velouté, and Chicken Stock and simmer for 20 minutes. Strain. Cool; complete with cream or non-dairy cream substitute and wine. Should not be frozen. *Yield:* 6–8 servings.

CHICKEN LIVER SOUP

2 ounces flour
4 tablespoons butter or margarine
1 quart Beef Stock*
10 ounces chicken livers, finely chopped
Pinch pepper
Dash Tabasco
¼ cup dry sherry

Make roux from flour and butter or margarine. Cook on a slow fire until golden brown. Add Beef Stock and stir constantly while cooking for 15 minutes. Add chicken livers and cook for another 10 minutes. Add pepper and Tabasco. The soup can be frozen at this stage. Complete with sherry. *Yield:* 6–8 servings.

CLAM CHOWDER

1 medium onion, diced
2 celery stalks, diced
1 medium green pepper, diced
Whites 1 leek, diced
¼ bay leaf
1 sprig fresh or pinch dried thyme
2 cups water
12 clams
1 quart water for steaming clams
1 large potato, diced
2 tablespoons arrowroot starch, cornstarch, or potato
  starch diluted in 2 tablespoons cold water
½ pint cream or non-dairy cream substitute

Cook onion, celery, green pepper, leek, bay leaf, and thyme
in 2 cups of water until the water is reduced to half its volume.
Wash the clams and steam them in 1 quart of water until they
open, about 5 to 10 minutes. Remove the clams and add the
liquid from cooking them to the vegetables. Add the potatoes
and cook until done, about 20 minutes. Thicken the soup with the
starch and water mixture and add the clam meat. The soup can
be frozen at this stage. Complete with cream or non-dairy cream
substitute. *Yield:* 6–8 servings.

CREAM OF CUCUMBER SOUP

2 pounds cucumbers, sliced
2 tablespoons butter or margarine
Water
1 pint Basic Cream Sauce*
2 cups milk or non-dairy milk substitute
Salt and pepper to taste
½ cup cream or non-dairy cream substitute
2 tablespoons Worcestershire sauce

Peel and remove seeds from the cucumbers and cook in the butter or margarine for a few minutes. Add water to cover and cook for 10 minutes. Add Cream Sauce and milk or non-dairy milk substitute and simmer for 30 minutes. Strain. Add salt, pepper, cream or non-dairy cream substitute and Worcestershire sauce. This soup can also be served cold, but in that event it should be thinned with cream or milk or a non-dairy substitute. Should not be frozen. *Yield:* approximately 6–8 servings.

LENTIL SOUP BAVARIAN STYLE

½ pound lentils
1 carrot
Whites 1 leek
2 celery stalks
1 medium onion
4 slices lean bacon or ham
1 quart water
½ tablespoon salt
4 tablespoons catsup
¼ cup dry sherry
2 skinless wieners, cooked and thinly sliced (optional)

Wash and soak the lentils for about 2 hours in warm water. Dice finely the carrot, whites of the leek, celery, and onion and fry them with the bacon or ham for about 10 minutes. Add the lentils, water, and salt and simmer for 1½ hours, or until lentils are done. Complete with catsup and sherry and garnish with the wieners. Can be frozen. *Yield:* 6–8 servings.

MARROW BEAN SOUP

 ½ pound marrow beans
 1 carrot
 Whites 1 leek
 1 medium onion
 2 celery stalks
 ¼ pound ham, finely diced
 1 quart water
 ½ tablespoon salt
 2 medium-sized fresh tomatoes, peeled, deseeded,
    and quartered

Wash beans thoroughly and soak in warm water for about 2 hours. Dice the carrot, whites of the leek, onion, and celery and fry with the ham for 10 minutes. If ham is very lean, a small amount of fat may be added. Add the drained beans, water, and salt and cook for about 1½ hours until the beans are done. Add the tomatoes and cook an additional 5 minutes. Can be frozen. *Yield:* 6–8 servings.

CREAM OF MUSHROOM SOUP

 2 cups chopped fresh mushrooms
 2 tablespoons butter or margarine
 1 pint Basic Cream Sauce*
 2 cups milk or non-dairy milk substitute
 Salt and pepper to taste
 ½ cup cream or non-dairy cream substitute
 1 tablespoon Worcestershire sauce
 ¼ cup dry sherry

Fry the mushrooms in the butter or margarine for a few minutes. Add the Cream Sauce and milk or non-dairy milk substitute and simmer for 30 minutes. Add remaining ingredients. Should not be frozen. *Yield:* 6–8 servings.

OATMEAL CREAM OF SPINACH SOUP

> ¼ *pound oatmeal*
> 1 *cup cold milk or non-dairy milk substitute*
> ¼ *pound fresh spinach, washed and chopped*
> 3 *cups boiling salted milk or non-dairy milk substitute*
> *Salt and pepper to taste*
> ½ *cup cream or non-dairy cream substitute*
> *Dash Cayenne pepper*

Dilute oatmeal with the cold milk or non-dairy milk substitute. Add the spinach and boiling salted milk or non-dairy milk substitute and simmer for 30 minutes. Strain, season, and complete with cream or non-dairy cream substitute and Cayenne pepper. Should not be frozen. *Yield:* 6–8 servings.

CHICKEN OKRA SOUP

> 1 *medium onion*
> 2 *leeks*
> 1 *green pepper*
> 1 *celery stalk*
> 1 *teaspoon butter or margarine*
> ¼ *pound smoked ham, diced*
> ¼ *pound raw chicken breasts, diced*
> 1 *quart Chicken Stock**
> ¼ *pound fresh okra, sliced*
> 1 *large fresh tomato, peeled, deseeded, and quartered*
> ¼ *cup cooked rice*

Chop the onion, whites of the leeks, green pepper, and celery in the butter or margarine. Add the ham, chicken, and Chicken Stock and simmer for 30 minutes. Add the okra and tomato and cook for an additional 10 minutes. Complete with rice. Can be frozen. *Yield:* 6–8 servings.

OYSTER OKRA SOUP

Proceed as for Chicken Okra Soup*, except substitute 2 dozen oysters for the ham and chicken.

FRENCH ONION SOUP

> 2 medium onions, sliced
> ¼ bay leaf
> 2 tablespoons butter or margarine
> 1 quart Beef Stock*
> 6–8 toast rounds sprinkled with Parmesan cheese

Fry the onions and bay leaf in the butter or margarine until golden brown. Add the Beef Stock and simmer for 30 minutes. Ladle into heavy soup cups, top with the toast rounds, and place under the broiler until brown, or if this is not possible, broil the cheese-sprinkled toast rounds before putting in soup. Can be frozen before adding the toast rounds. *Yield:* 6–8 servings.

PEA SOUP

> ½ pound split peas
> 2 stalks celery
> Whites 1 leek
> 1 medium onion
> ¼ pound ham, finely diced
> 1 quart water
> 1 tablespoon salt
> Pinch pepper
> 1 cup toast cubes fried in 2 tablespoons butter or
>   margarine (optional)

Wash the peas and soak them in warm water for about 2 hours. Dice finely the celery, leek, and onion and fry with the ham for about 10 minutes. If the ham is very lean, a small amount of fat may be added. Add the water, salt, and pepper and cook for 1½ hours, or until the peas are done. Can be frozen at this point. Before serving, garnish with the toast cubes and the butter or margarine. *Yield:* 6–8 servings.

CREAM OF PEA SOUP

Proceed as for Pea Soup*. Strain before adding toast cubes and add approximately ⅔ cup cream or non-dairy cream substitute until desired thickness is obtained. This soup should not be frozen. *Yield:* 8 servings.

POTAGE GERMAINE

3 tablespoons minute tapioca
*1 quart Beef Stock**
⅔ cup cream or non-dairy cream substitute
3 egg yolks
½ cup chopped parsley
1 cup cooked fresh peas

Add the tapioca to the Beef Stock and cook slowly for 20 minutes. Remove from heat. Combine the cream or non-dairy cream substitute and egg yolks and add to the soup. Garnish with the parsley and peas. This soup should not be frozen. *Yield:* 6–8 servings.

POTATO AND LEEK SOUP

Whites 2 leeks
1 medium onion
2 celery stalks
½ bay leaf
1 sprig fresh or pinch dried thyme
3 medium potatoes, sliced
1 quart water
1 tablespoon salt
1 cup cream or non-dairy cream substitute
2 tablespoons butter or margarine

Cut up coarsely the leeks, onion, and celery. Add bay leaf and thyme. Cook on very low fire for 10 minutes. Add potatoes, water, and salt and cook for about 1 hour. Strain. Complete with cream or non-dairy cream substitute and butter or margarine. This soup should not be frozen. *Yield:* 6–8 servings.

POTATO AND WATERCRESS SOUP

Proceed as for Potato and Leek Soup*, but add the stems of 1 bunch of watercress while cooking. When soup is completed, garnish with the leaves of the watercress that have been cooked for a few minutes with 1 tablespoon butter or margarine and ¼ cup water. This soup should not be frozen. *Yield:* 6–8 servings.

COLD VICHYSSOISE

Proceed as for Potato and Leek Soup*. When strained, dilute with cream or non-dairy cream substitute to the desired thickness. Add 2 tablespoons Worcestershire sauce, dash of Tabasco, and garnish with 1 tablespoon minced chives. This soup should not be too thick or highly seasoned. Should not be frozen. *Yield:* 6–8 servings.

COLD WATERCRESS SOUP

Proceed as for Cold Vichyssoise* except use Potato and Watercress Soup* instead of Potato and Leek Soup*. Should not be frozen. *Yield:* 6–8 servings.

SHRIMP BISQUE

1 carrot
1 small onion
1 celery stalk
2 tablespoons butter or margarine
¼ bay leaf
1 sprig fresh or pinch dried thyme
1 sprig parsley
20 shrimp, raw, peeled, and deveined
2 tablespoons brandy
2 tablespoons tomato purée
⅓ cup dry white wine
*1 quart Fish Velouté**
2 egg yolks
½ cup cream or non-dairy cream substitute
¼ cup dry sherry

Dice finely the carrot, onion, and celery and fry in butter or margarine. Add bay leaf, thyme, parsley, and shrimp and cook until shrimp turn pink. Add brandy and simmer a few minutes. Stir in the tomato purée, wine, and Fish Velouté. Cook for 20 minutes. Strain. Remove a few shrimp and dice them for garnish. Remove from fire and stir in egg yolks, cream or non-dairy cream substitute, and sherry. Once the eggs are put in do not return to the fire. This soup should not be frozen. *Yield:* 6–8 servings.

LOBSTER BISQUE

Proceed as for Shrimp Bisque* except use 2 cups of fresh or
frozen uncooked lobster for the shrimp.

CREAM OF SWEET POTATO SOUP

4 medium-sized sweet potatoes, baked
*2 cups Basic Cream Sauce**
2 cups milk or non-dairy milk substitute
Salt and white pepper to taste
Pinch nutmeg
1 tablespoon grated orange rind
1 cup steamed rice

Put sweet potatoes through a sieve. Add Cream Sauce and
milk or non-dairy milk substitute and cook over medium heat
for 10 minutes. Add remaining ingredients, using the rice for
garnish. This soup should not be frozen. *Yield:* 6–8 servings.

TOMATO SOUP

1 carrot
1 onion
1 celery stalk
Whites 1 leek
2 ounces salt pork, minced
¼ bay leaf
1 sprig fresh or pinch dried thyme
6 fresh tomatoes, quartered
1 teaspoon sugar
1 teaspoon salt
*1 pint Beef Stock**
*2 tablespoons arrowroot starch, cornstarch, or potato
    starch diluted with 2 tablespoons water*
*1½ cups steamed rice or 1 cup bread cubes fried
    in 2 tablespoons butter or margarine*

Dice the carrot, onion, celery, and leek and fry them in the salt pork with the bay leaf and thyme for about 10 minutes. Add tomatoes, sugar, salt, and Beef Stock. Cook slowly for 1 hour. Thicken with the diluted starch. Strain. Garnish with rice or bread cubes. Can be frozen. *Yield:* 6–8 servings.

VEGETABLE SOUP

Whites 2 leeks
2 celery stalks
1 medium onion
1 carrot
1 tablespoon butter or margarine
¼ bay leaf
1 sprig fresh or pinch dried thyme
*1 quart Beef Stock**
1 cup cooked peas or cooked rice or green beans or
    corn for garnish

Dice the leeks, celery, onion, and carrot. Fry them in the butter or margarine. Add bay leaf, thyme, and Beef Stock and cook on a low fire for about 1 hour. Garnish with the cooked vegetable or rice. Can be frozen. *Yield:* 6–8 servings.

CHAPTER 4

SALADS

Allergy Key: Salads come in endless shapes and forms and are capable of surviving innumerable substitutions. One main allergy problem is that of sensitivity to certain greens. Since sensitivity to one salad green generally does not carry over to other ones, a similar-looking or -tasting green can easily be substituted. Below is a list of salad greens to help make your substitution easier.

GREENS FOR SALADS

Boston or Betterhead Lettuce
Bibb or Limestone Lettuce
Head or Iceberg Lettuce
Romaine or Cos Lettuce
Leaf Lettuce
Grand Rapids Lettuce
Prize Head Lettuce
Oak Leaf Lettuce
Australian Lettuce
Cabbage
Chinese or Celery Cabbage
Celery
Celery Root or Celeriac

Chicory or Curly Endive
Belgian or French Endive
   or Witloof
Escarole
Field Salad
Garden Cress
Italian Fennel or Finocchio
Swiss Chard
Watercress
White Mustard
Sea Kale Leaves
Spinach

If you are careful and know what you are selecting, the following field greens can be used:

Dandelion Greens, Sorrel, and Winter Cress

VEGETABLE SALADS

BEAULIEU SALAD

½ pound cooked green beans
2 fresh tomatoes, quartered
1 small onion, sliced
½ cup Classic French Dressing*
4 anchovy fillets

Combine the first four ingredients and place on individual salad plates. Garnish with anchovy fillets. *Yield:* 4 servings.

BEET SALAD

8 beets
½ cup Classic French Dressing*
1 small onion, sliced
1 small bay leaf

Preheat oven to 350 degrees F. Bake beets until done. Skin, slice, and marinate them in the dressing with the onion and bay leaf. Serve on a bed of greens. *Yield:* 4 servings.

BRABANCONNE SALAD

2 stalks French or Belgian endive
2 medium-cooked potatoes
1 small onion, baked in the oven at 350 degrees F. until soft, approximately 25 minutes
½ cup Classic French Dressing*
Lettuce
6–8 sardines, skinless and boneless
2 medium fresh tomatoes, quartered

Cut coarsely the endive and cooked potatoes. Peel and chop the onion and add to the endive and potatoes. Dress with Classic French Dressing. Place individual portion on bed of lettuce. Garnish with sardines and tomato quarters. *Yield:* 4 servings.

RED CABBAGE SALAD

1 small red cabbage
½ cup Classic French Dressing*

Remove midribs of cabbage and cut in fine julienne strips. Marinate 3–4 hours in dressing. This salad will keep several weeks in the refrigerator. It can be used alone, or in combination with fresh greens such as escarole and endive. *Yield:* 4 servings.

CAULIFLOWER SALAD

1 whole cauliflower
Salted boiling water to cover cauliflower
½ cup Classic French Dressing*
1 teaspoon prepared mustard

Divide cauliflower in small parts; remove stems, and cook in salted boiling water to cover. Cook until tender but still firm. Remove from fire, drain and marinate 3–4 hours in Classic French Dressing to which the mustard has been added. *Yield:* approximately 4 servings.

CUCUMBER SALAD

2 cucumbers
Salt
½ cup sour cream or non-dairy sour cream substitute
1 tablespoon chopped chives

Peel cucumbers, remove seeds and slice thinly. Sprinkle with salt and let stand for 1 hour in refrigerator. Drain. Add sour cream or non-dairy sour cream substitute and chives and mix. *Yield:* 4 servings.

NAVY BEAN SALAD

1 pound navy beans
Salted water to cover beans
1 stalk celery
1 small onion, chopped
1 small carrot
½ bay leaf
½ cup Classic French Dressing*
¼ pound diced ham or wieners

Cook beans in salted water to cover. Add celery, onion, carrot, and bay leaf. Cook on slow fire for about 1½ hours, until done. Season with dressing. Add ham or wieners. This salad makes a fine hot weather meal. *Yield:* approximately 6 servings as side dish.

POTATO SALAD

2 pounds potatoes
Salted water to cover potatoes
1 small onion, chopped
1 hard-cooked egg, diced
1 stalk celery, chopped
¼ cup dry wine (any kind)
½ cup Mayonnaise*
Lettuce
4 strips pimento

Cook potatoes in their skins in boiling water to cover until tender. Peel and dice potatoes. Add remaining ingredients (except lettuce and pimento) and mix gently. Serve on lettuce. Garnish with pimento. *Yield:* approximately 6 servings.

PRINCESS SALAD

    4 pieces romaine
    1 fresh tomato
    16 pieces, approximately, fresh, canned, or frozen
      asparagus
    4 tablespoons Mayonnaise*
    4 strips pimento

Place a leaf of romaine lettuce on a salad plate. Add a large tomato slice. Place 4 asparagus spears on tomato slice on top of the lettuce: place 1 tablespoon Mayonnaise on top of the asparagus and decorate with pimento. *Yield:* 4 servings.

REGENT SALAD

    1 cup julienne-cut white meat of chicken
    1 cup julienne-cut ham
    1 cup julienne-cut beef tongue
    1 cup mushrooms sliced into strips
    1 cup French dressing, either American Style* or
      Classic*
    Lettuce
    For garnish: 1 cup artichoke hearts, olives, capers,
      and 4 fresh tomatoes, quartered

Marinate the chicken, ham, beef tongue, and mushrooms separately in French Dressing. Place on lettuce leaves in individual portions. Garnish with artichoke hearts, olives, capers, and tomato quarters. *Yield:* approximately 6 servings as main dish; 8 as a side dish.

TOMATO SALAD

4 large firm fresh tomatoes
2 cups of any of the following mixed with
Mayonnaise*: diced chicken, tuna fish, crab meat,
lobster or shrimp; or plain cottage cheese

Dip tomatoes in hot water and remove skins. Slice off the tops and hollow out the insides. Stuff each tomato with ½ cup of one of the suggested fillings. *Yield:* 4 servings.

COOKED VEGETABLE SALAD

1 pound fresh vegetables
1 cup salted boiling water
1 teaspoon chopped parsley
1 teaspoon prepared mustard
¾ cup Classic French Dressing*

Cook vegetables in water, covered, until done but still firm. Drain. Add parsley and mustard to dressing and add to vegetables. *Yield:* approximately 4 servings.

VINAIGRETTE SALAD

1 pound cooked artichokes, asparagus, beets, broccoli,
carrots, cauliflower, or leeks, prepared as for Cooked
Fresh Vegetables*
1 cup Vinaigrette Dressing*

Mix vegetables and Vinaigrette Dressing and refrigerate for 2–4 hours before serving. Serve as a salad. *Yield:* 4 servings.

WATERCRESS SALAD

   1 bunch watercress
   1 hard-cooked egg, chopped
   ½ cup Classic French Dressing*

Wash and drain watercress; cut stems off. Mix with egg and dressing. *Yield:* approximately 4 servings.

WESTPHALIAN SALAD

   1 cup diced cooked potatoes
   1 cup peeled diced apples
   1 cup chopped sweet pickles
   1 cup wine-marinated herring
   2 cups Mayonnaise*
   1 cup sour cream or non-dairy sour cream substitute
   2 hard-cooked eggs, sliced
   2 cooked beets, sliced

Mix the first six ingredients together. Garnish with the sliced eggs and beets. *Yield:* approximately 8 servings.

FRUIT SALADS

FRESH FRUIT SALAD

   1 quart assorted fresh fruits, such as melons, cherries, grapes, sliced bananas, citrus fruits, and berries

Wash fruit and cut into bite-size pieces. Serve with following dressing:

SALADS

45

COMBINE:
1 cup Mayonnaise*
½ cup whipped cream or non-dairy whipped cream
   substitute
1 cup fruit juice
2 drops grenadine

Yield: 8 servings as side dish; 4 servings as main dish.

FROZEN FRUIT SALAD

1 quart fresh fruit (see above recipe for suggestions)
1 cup Mayonnaise*
1 cup whipped cream or non-dairy whipped cream
   substitute
Juice 1 lemon
Lettuce

Combine the first four ingredients. Place in a mold in freezer until solid. Unmold on bed of lettuce and garnish with fresh fruit. Yield: approximately 8 servings as side dish.

JELLIED SALADS

JELLIED CHERRY AND WINE SALAD

2 one-pound cans pitted Bing cherries in heavy syrup
2 cups boiling water
2 three-ounce packages strawberry gelatin
¾ cup sweet red wine
¾ cup juice from canned cherries

Drain cherries and place in a mold; add the boiling water to the gelatin. Stir and then add the wine and cherry juice. Pour gelatin liquid over the cherries in the mold to a depth of about ¼ inch. Refrigerate until jelled. Then add the remaining gelatin and refrigerate several hours until the whole mold is jelled. *Yield:* 16–20 servings.

JELLIED CIDER SALAD

1 ounce unflavored gelatin
1 cup cool cider
3 cups boiling cider
1 cup canned orange sections
1 cup unpeeled diced apples
1 cup chopped celery

Soften gelatin in 1 cup of cool cider. Add boiling cider and let cool until mixture begins to thicken; add remaining ingredients and mix completely. Refrigerate until firm. *Yield:* approximately 8 servings.

JELLIED CRANBERRY SALAD

1 pound fresh cranberries
1 lemon, unpeeled
1 orange, unpeeled
1½ cups sugar
1 ounce unflavored gelatin
½ cup cold water
½ cup chopped pecans (optional)

Put the cranberries, lemon, and orange through a coarse grinder. Add sugar and bring to a boil. Remove from fire; soften the gelatin in cold water and add to the fruit. Add pecans if desired. Place in a mold and refrigerate until firm. *Yield:* 8 servings.

JELLIED GINGER ALE SALAD

1 ounce unflavored gelatin
1 cup cold ginger ale
3 cups boiling ginger ale
1 cup diced dried figs
1 cup parboiled raisins
2 tablespoons finely chopped ginger

Soften gelatin in cold ginger ale. Add to the boiling ginger ale and let cool until mixture begins to thicken. Add remaining ingredients. Place in mold and refrigerate until firm. *Yield:* 8 servings.

JELLIED MINCEMEAT SALAD

1 ounce unflavored gelatin
1 cup cold water
½ cup sugar
1 tablespoon lemon juice
2 cups boiling water
1 cup orange juice
1 recipe Mincemeat (see Mincemeat Pie* recipe)

Add gelatin to cold water. Add remaining ingredients one at a time, stirring until thoroughly mixed. Pour into mold and chill. Can be used as a salad or as a dessert. *Yield:* 10–12 servings.

JELLIED MANDARIN ORANGE SALAD

2 one-pound cans mandarin oranges
2 three-ounce packages orange gelatin
1½ cups boiling water
1 pint orange sherbet

Drain liquid from oranges thoroughly. Line bottom of a mold with the oranges. Dissolve gelatin in boiling water in a large bowl. Cool to lukewarm. Add almost completely melted sherbet to the gelatin; beat with electric mixer at slow speed until completely mixed. Pour over oranges in mold. Chill in refrigerator until firm.

It is important to have the original gelatin and water mixture cooled sufficiently so that the sherbet will not separate after the two are mixed together. *Yield:* 16–20 servings.

JELLIED TOMATO AND CUCUMBER SALAD

1 ounce unflavored gelatin
1 cup cold tomato juice
2 cups boiling tomato juice
1 teaspoon salt
1 tablespoon Worcestershire sauce
¼ teaspoon celery salt
2 cups chopped cucumbers, well drained

Soften gelatin in cold tomato juice. Add all remaining ingredients except cucumbers. Cool until mixture thickens, then stir in the cucumbers. Place in mold and refrigerate until firm. *Yield:* 8 servings.

JELLIED VEGETABLE SALAD

1 ounce unflavored gelatin
1 cup cold Chicken Stock*
3 cups boiling Chicken Stock*
Juice 1 lemon
1 teaspoon salt
2 cups cooked mixed vegetables, well drained

Soften gelatin in cold Chicken Stock. Add all remaining ingredients except the vegetables. Cool until mixture thickens, then stir in the vegetables. Place in mold and refrigerate until firm. *Yield:* 8 servings.

CHAPTER 5

FRUITS

Allergy Key: Some people are allergic to specific fruits, such as oranges or lemons or grapefruit. Others are allergic to all fruits of a type, such as all citrus fruits. After you have determined which fruits you are allergic to, you may select the ones you can eat from the fruits listed below. Fruits can be eaten either alone or in combination with other fruits—your tastes, your imagination, and your allergies need be your only guides.

Some of the fruit recipes in this chapter will also benefit those who are allergic to corn sugar and additives in canned fruits.

If you have numerous vegetable allergies, you can substitute fruit dishes for a vegetable with your meal.

FRUITS

Apples
Apricots
Avocados
Bananas
Blackberries
Blueberries
Cherries—sweet and sour
Coconuts
Cranberries
Cucumbers
Currants—red, white, and
    black

Dates
Dewberries
Elderberries
Figs
Gooseberries
Grapefruit—white and
    pink
Grapes—purple, red,
    and white
Kumquats
Lemons
Limes

Loquats
Mangoes
Melons—cantaloupe, casaba,
  honeydew, Persian,
  Spanish, watermelon
Nectarines
Olives—green and black
Oranges
Papayas
Peaches

Persimmons
Pineapples
Plums
Pomegranates
Raspberries—red and black
Strawberries
Tangelos
Tangerines
Tomatoes

BAKED APPLES

4 medium-sized McIntosh apples
½ cup blanched raisins (for blanching see Toasted
  Nuts*)
¼ cup brown sugar
1 tablespoon butter or margarine
1 cup water

Preheat oven to 375 degrees F. Wash and core the apples. Peel off skin to one-third of the space from the top. Mix raisins and brown sugar and fill the apple centers with this mixture. Dot the top of the apples with butter or margarine. Place in a baking dish; add water to the dish and bake for 35 minutes until apples are soft. Serve hot or cold. *Yield:* 4 servings.

GLAZED FRUITS

4 cups peeled fruit, any kind desired, or rhubarb
1 cup sugar
½ cup water
1–2 teaspoons liquor, liqueur, wine, lime juice, or
  vanilla extract (optional)

All fruit should be washed and peeled. If using a citrus fruit, separate the sections so as not to break the skin. Other fruits should be halved or quartered or cut into relatively large pieces. Small fruits such as berries, cherries, and grapes should be left whole.

Dissolve the sugar in the water and bring to a stiff boil, about 5 minutes. Add the fruit and cook until tender. Do not overcook. Fruits with a high water content are cooked on a hot fire to prevent their becoming mashed.

If flavoring is desired, sprinkle over the fruit just before removing from the fire. *Yield:* about 1½ cups fruit.

HOME FRIED APPLES

 2 *tablespoons butter or margarine*
 6 *medium-sized cooking apples, cored and sliced*
 3 *tablespoons sugar*
 ½ *teaspoon cinnamon*

Melt butter or margarine in a skillet, preferably an iron one. Add apples, sugar, and cinnamon and cook over a medium heat for about 15 minutes until done. Turn over during cooking. *Yield:* 4–6 servings.

APPLESAUCE

 8 *green apples, cored and peeled*
 3 *tablespoons sugar*
 ½ *cup water*
 Grated rind 1 lemon or 1 orange

Place all ingredients in a saucepan. Cook over low heat for about 15 minutes until apples are completely tender. Strain and serve. *Yield:* 4–6 servings.

BROILED BANANAS

4 bananas, firm and not yet ripe
Cinnamon
Sugar
2 tablespoons butter or margarine

Preheat broiler. Peel bananas and place them in a broiling pan.
Sprinkle with cinnamon and sugar and dot the tops with butter or
margarine. Broil for 8 minutes. *Yield:* 4 servings.

CRANBERRY JELLY

1 pound cranberries
2 cups water
6 whole cloves
2 cups sugar
Pinch salt

Wash cranberries. Place them in a pot with water and cloves and
cook over medium heat until soft. Strain. Add sugar and salt,
return to fire, and cook for 3 minutes longer. Chill and serve.
Yield: 4 servings.

BROILED GRAPEFRUIT

1 large grapefruit
Dark brown sugar
Dash dry sherry or port wine (optional)

Preheat broiler. Cut grapefruit in half; loosen sections and remove seeds. Sprinkle top with sugar. Broil for 8 minutes. Remove
from broiler; add a dash of wine if desired and serve. *Yield:* 2
servings.

BROILED MELON

1 cantaloupe, casaba, honeydew, or Persian melon
3 tablespoons sugar
¼ teaspoon ground ginger
Dry sherry or port wine (optional)

Preheat broiler. Cut melon into slices 1 inch thick. Mix sugar and ginger and sprinkle over melon. Broil until golden. Remove from broiler; if desired, sprinkle wine over the slices and serve. *Yield:* 4 servings.

GLAZED FRESH PINEAPPLE

1 fresh pineapple
Sugar for dredging
2 tablespoons butter or margarine
Kirsch

Core and peel the pineapple and cut into slices 1 inch thick. Dredge the slices in sugar. Melt butter or margarine in a heavy, shallow skillet and skim off the scum, leaving the fat clarified. Cook the pineapple slices in the skillet over medium heat until lightly browned. Pour liquid from pan over slices when serving and sprinkle with Kirsch. *Yield:* 4–6 servings.

CHAPTER 6

VEGETABLES

Allergy Key: Since vegetables are usually not served in combination, your task in this area usually is to select those vegetables that are permitted in the allergy diet. The following are our suggestions for varying the vegetable diet of the allergic eater.

The recipes for French Fried Potatoes*, Julienne Potatoes*, and Potato Chips* will be of special interest to those who are allergic to oils and therefore cannot buy these items on the commercial market.

ARTICHOKES

> *4 artichokes*
> *1 lemon, quartered*
> *String to tie artichokes*
> *1 teaspoon salt*
> *Water to 3-inch depth in pot*
> *¼ pound melted butter or margarine or 1 cup*
>   *Hollandaise Sauce**

Cut the stem and the brown tops of the leaves off the artichokes; rub with lemon, especially the cut parts. If desired, tie the artichokes lengthwise and widthwise to prevent falling apart in cooking. Place in deep pot with salted water. Bring to boil, cover, reduce heat, and steam for 30 to 40 minutes until leaves pull off easily. Serve with melted butter or margarine or Hollandaise Sauce. *Yield:* 4 servings.

COOKED FRESH VEGETABLES

> *1 pound net weight cleaned and trimmed of any of*
> *the following vegetables:*
> *asparagus; beans—green and wax; beets; broccoli;*
> *brussels sprouts; cabbage—red, white, and savoy;*
> *carrots; cauliflower; celery; corn (use 4 ears);*
> *onions, small white; oyster plant; parsnips; peas;*
> *spinach; turnips; zucchini*
> *salted boiling water to cover*
> *butter or margarine*

Bring water to a boil, add vegetables, cover and reduce heat. Cook over a low fire until vegetables are just tender. Do not overcook. Serve with butter or margarine or in one of the ways listed below. *Yield:* 4 servings.

Note: In cooking corn on the cob, sugar may be used in place of salt.

AU GRATIN:

> *1 pound cooked vegetable*
> *1 cup Basic Cream Sauce**
> *⅛ cup grated cheese*

Preheat oven to 350 degrees F. Drain vegetable well. Place in baking dish. Cover with Cream Sauce and grated cheese. Bake for 15 minutes. *Yield:* 4 servings.

CREAMED:

> *1 pound cooked vegetable*
> *½–1 cup cream or non-dairy cream substitute*
> *Salt and pepper to taste*

Drain vegetable and place in a saucepan. Cover with cream or non-dairy cream substitute. Cook on a low fire for 3–4 minutes. Season and serve. *Yield:* 4 servings.

HOLLANDAISE:

1 pound cooked vegetable
1 cup Hollandaise Sauce*

Drain vegetable and while still hot, serve with Hollandaise Sauce. *Yield:* 4 servings.

MILANESE:

1 pound cooked vegetable
2 hard-cooked eggs, chopped
⅛ cup grated Parmesan cheese
¼ pound butter or margarine

Drain vegetable well and place on a hot dish. Sprinkle with eggs and grated cheese. Melt butter until sizzling and turning brown. Pour over vegetable. *Yield:* 4 servings.

BRAISED VEGETABLES

1 tablespoon minced onion
4 strips bacon, cut into 1-inch pieces
1 pound cooked cabbage (red, white, or savoy),
celery, escarole, lettuce, sorrel, spinach, or Swiss
chard (see Cooked Fresh Vegetables* for
preparation)
Beef* or Chicken Stock* to cover
Salt and pepper to taste

Place onion and bacon in the bottom of a saucepan. Add well-drained vegetables and remaining ingredients. Cook covered over a slow fire for 30 minutes. *Yield:* 3 servings.

FRIED VEGETABLES

1 pound cooked cauliflower, onions, oyster plant,
   parsnips, turnips, or zucchini (see Cooked
   Fresh Vegetables*)
1 pound uncooked eggplant or tomatoes
Salt and pepper to taste
Flour (any kind) for dredging
Butter, margarine, or oil for cooking

Slice vegetables ½ inch thick or cut into wedges. Season with salt and pepper; dredge in flour and fry in butter, margarine, or oil until golden brown. *Yield:* 4 servings.

GLAZED VEGETABLES

1 pound net weight cleaned and trimmed of any of
   the following vegetables:
asparagus; carrots; leeks; mushrooms; onions, small
   white; parsnips; peas; rutabaga; butternut squash;
   summer squash; turnips; zucchini
4 tablespoons butter or margarine
Salt and pepper to taste
Water to cover
1 tablespoon chopped onion, bay leaf, or thyme or,
1 garlic clove, chopped (optional), or, for carrots
   and peas,
1 tablespoon sugar or 1½ tablespoons honey

Cut vegetables into bite-size pieces. Place all ingredients in a pot and cook over a hot fire until three-quarters of the liquid is evaporated. The vegetables should then be done. Serve hot. *Yield:* 4 servings.

DRIED VEGETABLES

1 pound of any of the following dried vegetables:
black beans; lima beans; navy beans; red kidney
*   beans; flageolets; lentils; peas*
1 medium carrot, sliced in large pieces
1 stalk celery, sliced in large pieces
1 medium onion, diced
Salted water to cover

Put all ingredients into a pot and bring to a boil. Reduce heat, cover pot, and simmer until done, about 1½ hours.

If the vegetables seem old, that is, unusually dehydrated and the skins shrunk, soak in warm water for 2 hours before cooking. Dried vegetables can be served Au Gratin*, Creamed*, Milanese*, or Braised*, using salt pork in place of bacon if desired, with Tomato Sauce* or cold in salads. *Yield:* 4 servings.

CREAMED BEAN SPROUTS

*2 cups Basic Cream Sauce**
2 cups cooked or canned bean sprouts (available in
*   Chinese food stores or specialty food stores)*
Salt and pepper to taste
¼ cup dry sherry

Bring Cream Sauce to a boil. Add bean sprouts and simmer over a slow fire for 10 minutes. Add salt, pepper, and dry sherry. Serve hot. *Yield:* 4 servings.

SAUTEED MUSHROOMS

Mushrooms are in reality an edible fungus but we have classed them as a vegetable for convenience.

2 cups sliced or quartered white mushrooms
2 tablespoons butter or margarine
1 tablespoon chopped green onion
¼ teaspoon salt
Pinch pepper

Rinse mushrooms thoroughly under running water and wipe dry with a cloth. Slice off the tip of the stem. Slice or quarter them and fry in hot melted butter or margarine for 5 minutes. Add remaining ingredients and fry for about 3 minutes longer. Serve as garnish for meats, vegetables, and eggs or in recipes as called for. *Yield:* approximately 1 cup.

FRENCH FRIED ONION RINGS

2 large onions sliced crosswise ⅛ inch thick
2 eggs
Salt to taste
3 tablespoons milk or non-dairy milk substitute
Flour for dredging (any kind)
Fat (any kind) at 170 degrees F. (the quantity of fat
 should be seven times the volume of the onions)

Separate onions carefully into rings. Beat eggs, salt, and milk or non-dairy milk substitute together. Dip onion rings in egg batter, then dredge in flour and fry in deep fat until brown. Use as garnish. *Yield:* approximately 2 cups.

SMOTHERED ONIONS

2 large onions, any kind
2 tablespoons butter or margarine
Salt and pepper to taste
Paprika

Mince onion. Melt butter or margarine in a heavy skillet. Add onion, salt, and pepper, and sprinkle paprika over the top. Cook over a slow fire until done, about 15 minutes. Use as garnish. *Yield:* approximately 1 cup.

BAKED POTATOES

4 medium potatoes
Butter, margarine, or oil for rubbing on skin
Butter or margarine or sour cream or non-dairy cream
   substitute flavored with crumbled bacon or chopped
   chives

Preheat oven to 425 degrees F. Scrub potatoes and grease the skins so they don't crack while baking. Bake for about 1 hour until completely soft on the inside when pierced. Serve with butter, margarine, or sour cream mixture. *Yield:* 4 servings.

BOILED POTATOES

4 medium potatoes, peeled
Salted water to cover
2 tablespoons butter or margarine
Chopped parsley

Boil potatoes in salted water for about 35 minutes, until completely tender. Drain off water. Return pan to fire long enough to

dry the potatoes, being careful not to burn them. Add the butter
or margarine and sprinkle with chopped parsley. *Yield:* 4 servings.

AU GRATIN POTATOES

> *4 medium potatoes*
> *Salted boiling water to cover*
> *1 cup 18 per cent cream (coffee cream) or non-dairy*
> *   cream substitute*
> *Salt and pepper to taste*
> *¼ cup cheese, crumbled, any kind you prefer*
> *2 tablespoons butter or margarine*

Preheat oven to 375 degrees F. Cook the potatoes in their skins
in salted boiling water for about 35 minutes, until completely
tender. Drain off water. Peel and dice. Combine cream or non-
dairy cream substitute, salt, and pepper with potatoes, and place
in baking dish. Sprinkle top with cheese and dot with butter or
margarine. Bake for 15 minutes. *Yield:* 4–6 servings.

FRENCH FRIED POTATOES

> *6 medium potatoes*
> *Salted boiling water to cover*
> *Fat (any kind) at 350 degrees F. (the quantity of fat*
> *   should be seven times the volume of the potatoes)*
> *Salt*

Peel potatoes and slice lengthwise in quarter-inch strips. Place
in boiling water for 3 minutes. Drain and wipe potato strips dry
with a cloth. Fry in deep fat until done, about 6 minutes. Remove
potatoes from fat and reheat fat to 350 degrees F. (it will have
cooled down in frying). Plunge potatoes into fat again and fry
until potatoes are brown and crisp. Remove potatoes from fat.
Salt and serve. *Yield:* 4–6 servings.

JULIENNE POTATOES

Proceed as for French Fried Potatoes* except cut potatoes in thin strips like matchsticks.

HASHED BROWN POTATOES

4 medium potatoes
Salt to taste
4 tablespoons butter or margarine for frying (more
    may be needed if potatoes are mealy)

Cook potatoes as for Au Gratin Potatoes*. Peel and dice. Add salt and fry in shallow frying pan until brown. *Yield:* 4–5 servings.

HASHED CREAMED POTATOES

4 medium potatoes
1 cup 18 per cent cream (coffee cream) or non-dairy
    cream substitute (more may be needed if potatoes
    are mealy)
Salt and pepper to taste
2 tablespoons butter or margarine

Cook potatoes as for Au Gratin Potatoes*. Peel and dice. Combine potatoes, cream or non-dairy cream substitute, and salt and pepper. Cook over medium heat until mixture has reached a creamy blend, about 5 minutes after reaching boiling point. Add butter or margarine and serve. *Yield:* 4–6 servings.

HOME FRIED POTATOES

>   4 medium potatoes
>   Salt to taste
>   4 tablespoons butter or margarine for frying (more
>   may be needed if potatoes are mealy)

Cook potatoes as for Au Gratin Potatoes*. Peel and slice ⅛ inch thick. Season with salt and fry in butter or margarine until brown. *Yield:* 4–6 servings.

LYONNAISE POTATOES

Proceed as for Home Fried Potatoes*, but add 3 tablespoons of Smothered Onions*.

MASHED POTATOES

>   4 medium potatoes
>   Salted water to cover
>   4 tablespoons melted butter or margarine
>   1 cup hot milk or non-dairy milk substitute
>   Salt and white pepper to taste

Peel potatoes and split them in half. Boil in salted water for 25 minutes or until completely tender. Drain water and return pot to the fire for a few minutes until the potatoes are dry. Mash with a potato masher; add remaining ingredients and whip until fluffy. *Yield:* 4–6 servings.

INSTANT MASHED WHITE OR SWEET POTATOES

There are several instant mashed potato products on the market now, including a sweet potato. These can be reconstituted according to directions by using milk, non-dairy milk substitutes, or fruit juices instead of water.

OVEN BROWNED POTATOES

12 small potatoes
Salted water to cover
Roasting meat

Peel the potatoes and place them in the water. Bring water to a boil and boil for 10 minutes. Remove potatoes and place them in the pan with whatever meat you are roasting for the last 30 minutes of roasting time. *Yield:* 4 servings.

POTATO CHIPS

6 medium potatoes
1 tablespoon salt
2 quarts cold water
Fat (any kind) at 350 degrees F. (the quantity of the fat
    should be seven times the quantity of the potatoes)
Salt to taste

Peel the potatoes and slice them as thin as possible. Add salt and potato slices to the water and soak for 2 hours. Drain well and place potatoes in the hot fat. Fry until crisp, remove from fat, salt and serve. *Yield:* 4–6 servings.

POTATO PANCAKES

6 *medium potatoes*
3 *eggs*
2 *tablespoons chopped green onions*
1 *teaspoon salt*
1 *tablespoon wheat or barley flour, or*
1 *teaspoon arrowroot starch, cornstarch, or potato
   starch, diluted in a small amount of cold water*
3–5 *tablespoons butter or margarine*

Peel and grate the potatoes. Add remaining ingredients, except
butter or margarine, and blend well. Melt the butter or margarine
in a frying pan and drop potato batter with a tablespoon into the
pan. Brown on both sides and serve. *Yield:* 4–6 servings.

BAKED SWEET POTATOES

4 *medium sweet potatoes*
Butter or margarine

Preheat oven to 375 degrees F. Scrub potatoes and bake them
for 45 minutes, until tender. Serve with butter or margarine. *Yield:*
4 servings.

WHIPPED SWEET POTATOES

1¾ *cups cooked sweet potatoes (cooked as in
   Mashed Potatoes*)*
¼ *cup milk or non-dairy milk substitute*
2 *tablespoons butter*
¼ *cup brown sugar*
1 *egg (optional)*
¼ *teaspoon vanilla*
¼ *teaspoon nutmeg*
6 *marshmallows*

Preheat oven to 350 degrees F. Whip the potatoes in electric mixer, adding remaining ingredients (except marshmallows) gradually. Mix to a smooth consistency. Place in ungreased casserole. Bake about 20 minutes, until hot throughout. Remove from oven and dot the top with marshmallows and return to oven for about another 5 minutes, until the marshmallows are browned and mostly melted. *Yield:* 4–6 servings.

BAKED SQUASH

1 medium-sized acorn or sultan squash
2 tablespoons butter or margarine
Salt and pepper to taste

Preheat oven to 350 degrees F. Cut squash into quarters. Remove seeds. Place squash skin side down on a baking dish. Dot top with butter, season, and bake 30–35 minutes until done. *Yield:* 4 servings.

BROILED TOMATOES

3 or 4 medium fresh tomatoes
Salt and pepper to taste
Flour (any kind) for dredging

Preheat broiler. Slice tomatoes ½ inch thick. Season and dredge in flour. Place on pan under broiler for 2–3 minutes. Carefully turn slices over on the other side with a spatula. Broil another 2–3 minutes and serve. *Yield:* 4 servings.

BROILED EGGPLANT

Substitute eggplant for the tomatoes and proceed as for Broiled Tomatoes*.

STEWED TOMATOES

4 medium fresh tomatoes
Salt and pepper to taste
2 tablespoons butter or margarine
Water to cover

Blanch the tomatoes in very hot water for 1 minute. Remove skin and seeds and cut into quarters. Place in pan with the remaining ingredients and cook uncovered over a low fire for about 5 minutes until tomatoes are thoroughly cooked. *Yield:* 4 servings.

CHAPTER 7

NOODLES, PASTA, AND RICE

Allergy Key: The recipes in this chapter offer wonderful substitutes for potatoes, quite a common allergy. They also offer an opportunity for variations in a potentially monotonous diet. There are some recipes for wheat-free noodles for the noodle or spaghetti lovers. The rice dishes can be used for those who have wheat allergies and therefore cannot eat pasta.

EGGDROP FOR SOUP
NO MILK—NO WHEAT—NO CORN

> 1 egg
> 2 tablespoons arrowroot starch, potato starch, or
>   cornstarch, diluted in 2 tablespoons water
> Dash salt

Combine all ingredients and beat until smooth. Drop from a spoon into boiling soup. Reduce heat, cover, and cook for additional 5–10 minutes. *Yield:* 4 servings.

NOODLES FOR SOUP OR SPAGHETTI—I
NO MILK—NO WHEAT—NO CORN

> 2 eggs
> ⅔ cup rye flour
> ⅔ cup barley flour
> Few dashes salt

Combine all ingredients; knead until dough is well mixed. Roll out on a floured board to thickness of a thin noodle. Let dry on board for about 30 minutes. Either slice this way or roll into a flat roll and slice to desired thickness. Spread noodles to dry for about 30 minutes. Store in an airtight container for a short time or freeze.

To cook, bring salted water to cover to a rolling boil; add noodles and simmer for 20 minutes or until tender. *Yield:* 4 servings.

NOODLES FOR SOUP OR SPAGHETTI—II
NO MILK—NO CORN

3¾ *cups wheat flour*
1 *tablespoon salt*
3 *whole eggs*
5 *egg yolks*
¼ *cup water*

Sift flour into mixing bowl. Hollow out the center and add remaining ingredients. Mix thoroughly and knead until dough is smooth. Cover with a dry cloth and let dough rest in a cool place for 2 hours.

Roll dough out on a floured board and let it rest for an hour before cutting into desired widths.

To cook, bring 2 quarts of salted water to a rolling boil. Add noodles and reduce heat. Simmer for about 20 minutes until noodles are tender. *Yield:* 4 servings.

NOODLES FOR SOUP OR SPAGHETTI—III
NO MILK—NO WHEAT

2 *tablespoons butter or margarine*
4 *eggs*
2 *teaspoons cornstarch*
Dash salt

Preheat oven to 300 degrees F. Melt butter in large saucepan; beat eggs, cornstarch, and salt in a bowl until thoroughly mixed, then add to melted butter in saucepan. Cook at low heat on top of stove for 5–8 minutes; put in oven for 12–15 minutes, until all the egg is cooked. Let cool, then cut into strips of the desired width. *Yield:* 4 servings.

RICE PILAFF

1 small onion, chopped
1 cup rice, uncooked
4 tablespoons butter or margarine
2 cups Beef Stock* or Chicken Stock*

Preheat oven to 350 degrees F. Fry onion and rice in butter or margarine for about 2 minutes. Add the stock and place in oven for about 20 minutes, until all the liquid is absorbed. Serve immediately. *Yield:* 8–10 servings.

Note: If the pilaff is to be cooked over a stove, rather than in the oven, maintain medium heat and add 10–15 minutes to the cooking time.

RICE RING

¼ cup butter or margarine
1 cup cooked rice (any kind will do—the commercial
    packages of rice and seasonings are also very good)
½ teaspoon nutmeg
1 cup chopped onion
Mushrooms (optional)

Preheat oven to 350 degrees F. Melt butter or margarine and add to the cooked rice. Add the remaining ingredients and place

in a well-greased ring mold. Set the mold in a pan of hot water
and bake for 20 minutes, or until hot throughout.

To unmold, loosen the edges of the mold with a knife and invert
the mold on a platter; it may not come out perfectly, but it repairs
well. *Yield:* 4 servings.

RICE ANDALUZ

  1 recipe Rice Pilaff*
  Pinch saffron
  2 medium fresh tomatoes—peeled, deseeded, and
     chopped

While cooking the Rice Pilaff, add the saffron. When finished
cooking, add the tomatoes and serve. *Yield:* 4–6 servings.

CURRIED RICE

Proceed as for Rice Pilaff*, but add 1 teaspoon curry powder
when frying the onions and rice. *Yield:* 4–6 servings.

CREOLE RICE

  1 medium onion, minced
  1 small green pepper, chopped
  4 large mushrooms, sliced
  4 tablespoons butter or margarine
  1 cup rice, uncooked
  2 cups Chicken* or Beef Stock*
  2 medium fresh tomatoes, peeled, deseeded, and
     chopped

Preheat oven to 350 degrees F. Sauté the onion, green pepper,
and mushrooms in the butter or margarine for a few minutes until

partially cooked. Add rice and stock. Cover and place in the oven for about 18 minutes, until all the liquid is absorbed. Remove from oven, add the tomatoes and serve. *Yield:* 4–6 servings.

ITALIAN RISOTTO

   1 recipe Rice Pilaff*
   2 tablespoons grated Gruyère cheese
   2 tablespoons grated Parmesan cheese
   ½ cup hot Chicken* or Beef Stock*

Prepare Rice Pilaff. When finished, add remaining ingredients and serve. *Yield:* 6 servings.

SHRIMP PILAFF

   1 medium onion, minced
   1 large green pepper, chopped
   2 cups sliced fresh mushrooms
   6 tablespoons butter or margarine
   4 medium fresh tomatoes, peeled, deseeded, and
      chopped
   1 cup rice, uncooked
   3 cups Fish* or Chicken Stock*
   1 pound peeled raw shrimp
   Salt and pepper to taste

Preheat oven to 350 degrees F. Sauté onion, green pepper, and mushrooms in butter or margarine for a few minutes until partially cooked. Add remaining ingredients. Cover and bake for 25 minutes, until all the liquid is absorbed. *Yield:* 8 servings.

CHAPTER 8

EGG DISHES

Allergy Key: These recipes will aid in providing variety in a restricted diet that might become very monotonous. They will be very useful to those with allergies to meats or fish. Although eggs are usually thought to be breakfast and luncheon dishes, many of the egg recipes in this chapter can also be used as a dinner entreé if served in more substantial portions along with vegetables and a salad.

Note: Eggs should not be *over*-cooked or the whites will toughen.

BAKED EGGS

8 tablespoons cream or non-dairy cream substitute
4 four-ounce china custard cups
4 eggs
Salt
White pepper

Preheat oven to 350 degrees F. Heat the cream or non-dairy cream substitute until hot, but not boiling. Place 2 tablespoons of this liquid in each custard cup. Break 1 egg into each cup; top with a dash of salt and white pepper on each. Place in a baking pan filled with 1–2 inches of hot water. Bake in oven for about 10 minutes, until the whites are set. Wipe the dishes clean and serve. Cold cream or non-dairy cream substitute may be used without harm to the finished product, but increase the baking time to about 20 minutes, or until the whites are set. *Yield:* 4 servings.

SOFT-COOKED EGGS

Salted cold water to cover
Eggs at room temperature

Bring pot of water with eggs in it to a boil. Remove pot from
fire. Let eggs stand in hot water—2 minutes for medium-sized eggs
and 3 minutes for large eggs. Remove and serve immediately.
Allow 1 or 2 eggs per person.

HARD-COOKED EGGS

Proceed as for Soft-Cooked Eggs* but let the eggs boil 8 minutes
for medium-sized eggs and 10 minutes for large eggs. Remove eggs
and place in cold water. Peel and serve. Allow 1 or 2 eggs per
person.

FRIED EGGS

1 tablespoon butter or margarine
Salt and pepper to taste
2 eggs

Melt the butter or margarine in a 6-inch skillet. Put salt and
pepper in bottom of pan so that egg yolks will not discolor. Carefully break the eggs and slide them into the pan. Cook over a slow
fire until egg whites are set to a milky white color. *Yield:* 1 or 2
servings.

SCRAMBLED EGGS

1½ tablespoons butter or margarine
4 eggs
Salt and pepper to taste
2 tablespoons cream or non-dairy cream substitute

Melt 1 tablespoon butter or margarine in skillet. Beat eggs with salt and pepper in a bowl. Pour into frying pan. Cook eggs over low heat, stirring with a wooden spoon until they are a creamy soft solid. Remove from fire and add remaining butter or margarine and the cream or non-dairy cream substitute. Fold gently into the eggs and serve. *Yield: 2–4 servings.*

SHIRRED EGGS

Salt and pepper to taste
Individual baking dishes, greased
2 eggs per serving

Preheat oven to 300 degrees F. Put salt and pepper on bottom of baking dishes to keep the yolks from spotting. Break 2 eggs into each dish. Bake for about 10 minutes, until the whites are set.

Some suggested accompaniments for the above egg recipes are bacon, Canadian bacon, grilled ham, shirred Lamb Kidney Saute*, Sauteed Chicken Livers*, Sausages*, Asparagus*, Sautéed Mushrooms*, French Fried Onion Rings*, French Fried Potatoes*, sliced tomatoes, and Tomato Sauce*.

OMELET

1 tablespoon butter or margarine
Pinch salt
Pinch white pepper
3 eggs, slightly beaten
2 tablespoons cream or non-dairy cream substitute
(optional)

Melt the butter in an omelet pan (or a frying pan no more than 6–7 inches in diameter). Season the eggs, add cream or non-dairy cream substitute if desired, beat well, and pour into the pan. Cook over moderate heat until the eggs are set, lifting the eggs with a fork or spatula several times to permit the uncooked eggs to seep down against the pan and solidify. When mixture is set but still creamy on top, cook about half a minute longer. Roll and turn the omelet over on a warm plate, unless the omelet is to be filled. The fillings should be added while the eggs are still in the pan. After filling, roll with the aid of a fork or spatula. Remove from the pan to a warm plate and serve. *Yield:* 2–4 servings.

FILLED OMELETS

If an omelet is to be filled, it should be cooked until firm so that the liquid of the eggs does not mix with the filling.

Some popular fillings are diced cheese, Smothered Onions*, Creamed Bean Sprouts*, Creamed or Buttered Spinach*, Stewed Tomatoes*, Sautéed Mushrooms*, Creamed Crab Meat*, Lobster*, Shrimp*, or Tuna Fish*, Creamed Chicken*, Sautéed Chicken Livers*, Sweetbreads*.

If jelly, marmalade, or preserves are used as a filling, sprinkle the top surface with granulated sugar and put under the broiler for a few minutes until glazed.

COUNTRY STYLE OMELET

> *2 tablespoons butter or margarine*
> *¼ cup minced ham*
> *¼ cup diced cooked potatoes*
> *Salt and pepper to taste*
> *3 eggs, well beaten*

Melt butter or margarine in a frying pan. Add minced ham and potatoes. Fry until potatoes are golden in color. Salt and pepper the eggs and pour into pan. Cook on low heat, lifting the edges to let the liquid eggs run to the bottom of the pan. When the eggs have cooked to a solid, slide onto a warm plate and serve. Do not roll. *Yield:* 2–4 servings.

SAVOYARDE OMELET

½ cup diced cooked potatoes
2 tablespoons butter or margarine
Salt and pepper to taste
3 eggs, well beaten
Thin strips Gruyère or Swiss cheese

Preheat oven to 300 degrees F. Fry diced potatoes in the butter or margarine. Season eggs and pour into pan. Top with cheese strips and bake in oven until eggs are set, about 3–4 minutes. *Yield:* 2–3 servings.

POACHED EGGS

Few dashes salt
2 tablespoons white vinegar
1 quart water
4 eggs

Add salt and vinegar to the water and bring it to a boil. Break eggs gently into the water, reduce heat, and let simmer until the egg yolks are completely covered with the whites, about 4 minutes. Remove from water with a perforated spoon, drain off excess water, and serve on rusk or toast if desired. *Yield:* 2–4 servings.

POACHED EGGS IN RED WINE

1 pint red wine (any kind), enough to cover eggs
when cooking
3 or 4 eggs
3 or 4 slices toast or rusk
1 tablespoon cornstarch for each pint wine used

Bring wine to a boil and poach eggs as in Poached Eggs*
Remove eggs and place on rusk or toast. Mix the cornstarch with
a little of the wine before mixing it into the whole pot of wine.
Mix well and pour as a sauce over the eggs. *Yield:* 3–4 servings.

POACHED EGG DISHES

AMERICAN:

Split a large tomato; sprinkle it with butter or margarine and
bread or cereal crumbs (any kind you are not allergic to); broil
under a low fire about 10 minutes; place a Poached Egg* on each
tomato half; cover with Smothered Onions* and serve.

ARTICHOKE:

Place Poached Egg* on well-drained large artichoke bottom;
cover with Hollandaise Sauce* and serve.

BENEDICT:

Toast a split English muffin; cover each muffin half with a slice
of grilled ham; top with a Poached Egg*; cover with Hollandaise
Sauce* and serve.

DELAMORE:

Fry medium-sized Crab Meat Cakes* or Codfish Cakes* until
golden brown; top each cake with a Poached Egg*; cover with
Tomato Sauce* and serve.

FLORENTINE:

Line bottom of baking dish with Creamed Spinach*; place Poached Eggs* on top of spinach; cover eggs with Mornay Sauce*; sprinkle with grated cheese and place under the broiler until glazed.

BROCCOLI:

Proceed as in Florentine*, above, except substitute broccoli spears for the spinach.

JUDIC:

Proceed as in Florentine*, above, but substitute Braised Lettuce* for the spinach.

GEORGETTE:

Cut off top of baked potato; scoop out to about 1 inch in depth; place Poached Egg* in the hollow; cover with Mornay Sauce* and place under the broiler until glazed.

À LA REINE:

Place diced Creamed Chicken* in baking dish; place Poached Eggs* on top; cover with Mornay Sauce*; sprinkle with grated cheese and place under the broiler until glazed.

BALTIMORE:

Proceed as in à la Reine*, above, but substitute Creamed Crab Meat* for Creamed Chicken* and add diced green and red peppers.

CHAPTER 9

CHEESE DISHES

Allergy Key: If you are not alergic to milk, cheese dishes are a wonderful substitute for meat and fish entrées. The recipes in this chapter can be used either for luncheon or dinner.

SWISS CHEESE FONDUE

1 pound coarsely grated imported Swiss cheese
1 tablespoon cornstarch
1 pint dry white wine
Pinch salt
Dash Cayenne pepper
4 tablespoons Kirsch
Small chunks French bread

Dust the Swiss cheese with the cornstarch; moisten with the wine; add salt and Cayenne pepper. Place in heavy saucepan and bring to a boil; remove from fire and add the Kirsch. Place in chafing dish and serve with bite-size crusty French bread using fondue forks for dipping the bread into the cheese. *Yield:* approximately 8 servings as appetizer, approximately 4 servings as main course.

CHEESE SOUFFLE

1½ cups Basic Cream Sauce*
½ cup grated Gruyère cheese
½ cup grated Cheddar cheese
Dash Cayenne pepper
Pinch grated nutmeg
5 eggs, separated

Preheat oven to 350 degrees F. Bring to a boil the Cream Sauce and both cheeses. Add Cayenne pepper and nutmeg. Blend in beaten egg yolks. Beat the egg whites until stiff. Gently fold them by hand into the cheese mixture. Pour into buttered 1-quart soufflé dish (oven-proof, straight-sided baking dish). Place in pan of hot water and bake for 45 minutes. *Yield:* 4–6 servings.

QUICHE LORRAINE

4 slices bacon
8 ounces coarsely grated Swiss cheese
1 unbaked 9-inch Pie Crust*
1 tablespoon arrowroot starch, cornstarch or potato starch
1 pint cold milk or non-dairy milk substitute
4 eggs
1 teaspoon salt
Dash nutmeg
Dash Cayenne pepper
½ cup half-and-half (milk and cream or non-dairy milk and cream substitutes)
1 tablespoon melted butter

Preheat oven to 450 degrees F. Cut each slice of bacon into 4 pieces; fry until done but not crisp; drain on paper towel. Sprinkle cheese and crumbled bacon in bottom of pie shell. Dissolve the starch in 3 tablespoons of the cold milk or non-dairy milk substitute and beat well with the eggs, salt, nutmeg, and Cayenne pepper. Scald the remaining milk or non-dairy milk substitute and the half-and-half and add to the egg mixture. Pour into the pie shell. Dribble melted butter on top. Bake in oven on the bottom rack for 10 minutes; reduce heat to 325 degrees F. and bake for an additional 25 minutes until the custard sets. Turn off oven heat and open oven door so as to let the quiche cool gradually in the oven (about 15 minutes). Serve warm.

Quiche Lorraine can be served in small slices as an appetizer, or a main course. *Yield:* approximately 8 servings as appetizer; approximately 4 servings as main course.

The trick of baking a perfect quiche is to keep it from weeping; by using a hot oven first and the cornstarch, weeping and tearing can be prevented.

INDIAN CHEESE SOUFFLE

1 quart milk or non-dairy milk substitute
1 teaspoon salt
⅔ cup cornmeal (white or yellow)
4 tablespoons butter or margarine
6 ounces grated white Cheddar cheese
5 eggs, separated
1 whole egg

Preheat oven to 350 degrees F. Place milk and salt in a saucepan and bring to a boil; sprinkle with the cornmeal. Bake in a buttered baking dish for 20 minutes. Remove from oven and place in mixing bowl with the butter or margarine, cheese, egg yolks, 1 whole egg, and stir until well blended. Beat egg whites until stiff. Gently fold them by hand into the cheese mixture. Pour into buttered 1-quart soufflé dish. Place in pan of hot water and bake at 350 degrees F. for 45 minutes. *Yield:* 4–6 servings.

WELSH RAREBIT

1 pound Cheddar cheese
1 teaspoon dry mustard
½ cup ale
4 thick slices buttered toast

Melt all the ingredients except the toast in a saucepan until the mixture bubbles. Place toast on warm dishes; pour on cheese mixture and serve. *Yield:* 4 servings.

GOLDEN BUCK

Proceed as for Welsh Rarebit*, but top each serving with a Poached Egg*.

CHAPTER 10

SAUCES AND DRESSINGS

Allergy Key: Many allergies can be catered to by judicious selection among the many recipes offered in this chapter. The basic sauces are presented with both wheat flour and starch recipes. A non-dairy milk substitute can be used in place of milk. Where a recipe calls for oil, any oil can be selected from the list in Chapter I. Where there is an allergy to seasonings, use the comprehensive herb list given in Chapter I for suggestions in making substitutions. None of these recipes use food preservatives, so all of them can be used by persons with that allergy. There are numerous recipes without eggs to enhance the egg-free diet. What better way to dress up a restricted diet than to serve it with an elegant sauce!

BASIC SAUCES

BASIC CREAM SAUCE WITH WHEAT FLOUR

Used as a sauce with meats, vegetables, and soups, and in compound sauces

    4 tablespoons butter or margarine
    ½ cup wheat flour
    1 quart milk or non-dairy milk substitute, scalded
    1 tablespoon salt
    ½ teaspoon white pepper
    1 small onion, chopped

Combine butter or margarine and flour in a small saucepan and cook for 5 minutes; cool. Add scalded milk or non-dairy milk substitute and blend well. Add seasonings and onion. Cook for 15 minutes on a slow fire. Strain and serve. Can be frozen. *Yield:* approximately 1 quart.

BASIC CREAM SAUCE WITH STARCH

Used as a sauce with meats, vegetables, and soups and in compound sauces

> ¼ cup arrowroot starch, cornstarch, or potato starch
> ¾ cup cold milk or non-dairy milk substitute
> 3¼ cups milk or non-dairy milk substitute, scalded
> 1 tablespoon salt
> ½ teaspcon white pepper
> 1 small onion, chopped

Dissolve the starch in the cold milk or non-dairy milk substitute. Add the hot milk or non-dairy milk substitute and blend well. Add seasonings and onion. Cook for 15 minutes on a slow fire. Strain and serve. Can be frozen. *Yield:* approximately 1 quart.

CHICKEN VELOUTE

Used for white meats, soups, and in compound sauces

Proceed as for Basic Cream Sauce with Wheat Flour* or Basic Cream Sauce with Starch* except substitute Chicken Stock* for the milk. Can be frozen.

FISH VELOUTE

Used for fish, soups, and in compound sauces

Proceed as for Basic Cream Sauce with Wheat Flour* or Basic Cream Sauce with Starch* except substitute Fish Stock* for the milk and add ½ cup dry white wine. Can be frozen.

BASIC BROWN SAUCE WITH WHEAT FLOUR

Used for meats and compound sauces

4 tablespoons butter or margarine
½ cup wheat flour
1 quart Beef Stock, hot*
½ tablespoon salt
*½ cup Tomato Sauce**
1 sprig fresh or pinch dried thyme
½ bay leaf

Combine butter or margarine and flour in a small saucepan and cook for 5 minutes; cool. Add the Beef Stock and blend well. Add all the other ingredients and boil for 25 minutes. Strain and serve. Can be frozen. *Yield:* approximately 1 quart.

BASIC BROWN SAUCE WITH STARCH

Used for meats and compound sauces

¼ cup arrowroot starch, cornstarch, or potato starch
*¾ cup cold Beef Stock**
*3¼ cups hot Beef Stock**
*½ cup Tomato Sauce**
½ tablespoon salt
1 sprig fresh or pinch dried thyme
½ bay leaf

Dissolve the starch in the cold stock. Add the hot stock and blend well. Add all the other ingredients and boil for 25 minutes. Strain and serve. Can be frozen. *Yield:* approximately 1 quart.

HOLLANDAISE SAUCE

Used for vegetables and fish

> *1 tablespoon salt*
> *1 teaspoon white pepper*
> *3 tablespoons vinegar*
> *2 tablespoons cold water*
> *8 egg yolks at room temperature*
> *1½ pounds butter or margarine, melted*
> *Juice 1 lemon*
> *Dash Cayenne pepper*

Place salt, white pepper, and vinegar in a saucepan and cook until one-half of the liquid volume has boiled off. Remove saucepan from fire and add cold water and the egg yolks. Put the mixture in a stainless steel or china bowl and set in a pan of hot water. Beat constantly (preferably with a wire whisk) until the mixture is the consistency of thick cream. Remove the mixture bowl from the hot water bath. Add the warm melted butter or margarine, a very small amount at a time, beating constantly until it is completely absorbed. Add lemon juice and Cayenne pepper and stir. Serve warm.

The sauce should be kept warm at all times or it will separate. Should not be frozen. *Yield:* approximately 1 quart.

TOMATO SAUCE

Used for meats and compound sauces

> *2 ounces salt pork*
> *5 pounds fresh tomatoes or 12 ounces tomato paste*

1 sprig or pinch dried thyme
½ bay leaf
1 garlic clove, chopped
1 celery stalk, diced
1 small onion, diced
1 medium carrot, diced
½ cup wheat flour or ¼ cup arrowroot starch, corn
   starch or potato starch
1 quart Beef Stock*, scalded
1 tablespoon salt
½ tablespoon pepper

Preheat oven to 350 degrees F. Fry the salt pork; when it is nearly melted add the tomatoes or tomato paste, thyme, bay leaf, garlic, celery, onion, and carrot. Simmer for a few minutes; add the flour or starch and mix thoroughly. Add the scalded Beef Stock and seasonings. Cover the pan and bake in the oven for 1 hour. Strain and serve. Can be frozen. *Yield:* approximately 2 quarts.

SMALL COMPOSITE SAUCES

BEARNAISE SAUCE

Used for red meats or broiled fish

2 tablespoons minced shallots
6 peppercorns, crushed
1 tablespoon fresh tarragon or ½ teaspoon dried
   tarragon leaves
Pinch salt
5 tablespoons vinegar
1 pint Hollandaise Sauce*
Dash Cayenne pepper
1 teaspoon chopped chervil or parsley

Place shallots, peppercorns, tarragon, salt, and vinegar in a small saucepan. Cook until one-third of the liquid has boiled off. Remove from fire; let cool. Add Hollandaise Sauce. Strain. Add Cayenne pepper and chervil or parsley.

Béarnaise Sauce should be kept warm. Temperature extremes of heat or cold will separate the sauce. Should not be frozen. *Yield:* approximately 1 pint.

BORDELAISE SAUCE

Used for beef

2 tablespoons chopped shallots or chives
1 cup dry red wine
Sprig fresh or pinch dried thyme
*1 pint Basic Brown Sauce**

Place shallots or chives, wine, and thyme in a saucepan. Cook until two-thirds of the liquid has boiled off. Add Brown Sauce. Boil for 10 minutes. Can be frozen. *Yield:* approximately 1 pint.

BUTTER SAUCE

Used for boiled meats

*1 pint Chicken Velouté**
4 egg yolks
3 tablespoons cream or non-dairy cream substitute

Bring the Chicken Velouté to a boil. Add the egg yolks mixed with the cream or non-dairy cream substitute. Remove from heat before the eggs and cream boil.

If sauce is intended for use on fish, replace the Chicken Velouté with Fish Velouté* and follow the same procedure. Should not be frozen. *Yield:* approximately 3 cups.

CAPER SAUCE

Used for boiled lamb shoulder and other boiled meats

> 1 tablespoon capers
> 1 pint Butter Sauce*

Add the capers to the Butter Sauce. Should not be frozen. *Yield:* approximately 1 pint.

CURRY SAUCE

Used for fish, shellfish, poultry, and eggs

> 4 tablespoons butter or margarine
> 1 small onion, chopped
> 1 celery stalk, minced
> 1 sprig fresh or pinch dried thyme
> ⅛ bay leaf
> 1 teaspoon curry powder
> 1 pint Chicken Velouté* or Fish Velouté*
> 3 tablespoons cream, non-dairy cream substitute
>   or coconut milk

Brown slightly in the butter or margarine, the onion, celery, thyme, and bay leaf. Add curry powder and Velouté. Cook for 10 minutes. Strain. Add the cream, non-dairy cream substitute or coconut milk. Can be frozen before cream is added. *Yield:* approximately 1 pint.

HERB SAUCE

Used for boiled fish

1 tablespoon chopped parsley
1 tablespoon chopped chives
*1 tablespoon chopped tarragon (½ teaspoon if using
dried leaves)*
1 pint Butter Sauce*

Add the seasonings to the sauce. Should not be frozen. *Yield:*
approximately 1 pint.

HORSERADISH SAUCE

Used for cold meats

2 tablespoons grated horseradish
*2 tablespoons fresh bread crumbs (from any kind of
bread)*
1 pint Basic Cream Sauce*
*2 tablespoons sour cream or non-dairy sour cream
substitute*
Juice 1 lemon

Add horseradish and bread crumbs to the Cream Sauce and cook
for 5 minutes. Remove from heat. Stir in the sour cream or non-dairy
sour cream substitute and lemon juice and serve. Should not be
frozen. *Yield:* approximately 1 pint.

MONTE CARLO SAUCE

Used for any meats or fish

2 tablespoons chopped onion

2 tablespoons oil
6 fresh tomatoes, peeled and deseeded
Salt and pepper to taste
1 clove garlic, crushed
½ pint Basic Brown Sauce*

Fry the onion in the oil until slightly brown. Cut up the tomatoes and add to onions. Add seasonings and Brown Sauce and simmer for 15 minutes. Can be frozen. *Yield:* approximately 1 pint.

MUSHROOM SAUCE—I

Used for beef

8 medium-size mushrooms, minced
1 tablespoon butter or margarine
1 tablespoon chopped onion
1 pint Basic Brown Sauce*
1 tablespoon dry sherry

Fry the mushrooms quickly in the butter or margarine. Add the remaining ingredients; heat and serve. Can be frozen before sherry is added. *Yield:* approximately 1 pint.

MUSHROOM SAUCE—II

Used for beef

1 tablespoon chopped onion
2 cups cut in half fresh mushrooms
3 tablespoons butter or margarine
½ cup Beef Stock*
3 tablespoons dry sherry

Sauté onions and mushrooms in butter or margarine for a few minutes. Add stock and cook until mushrooms are done. Remove from fire. Add sherry and serve. Can be frozen before sherry is added. *Yield:* approximately 1 pint.

MORNAY SAUCE

> 2 *tablespoons Parmesan cheese*
> 1 *cup Basic Cream Sauce**
> ½ *cup unsweetened whipping cream or non-dairy whipping cream substitute*

Add cheese to Cream Sauce and heat until cheese is melted. Add cream or non-dairy cream substitute and use as a topping as desired for vegetables, meat, fish, or eggs. Place under the broiler until glazed. *Yield:* 1½ cups.

MUSTARD SAUCE

Used for boiled meats and boiled fish

> 1 *pint Butter Sauce**
> 1 *teaspoon dry mustard*
> 1 *tablespoon prepared mustard*

Bring the Butter Sauce to just below a boil. Add the mustards and serve. Should not be frozen. *Yield:* approximately 1 pint.

MUSTARD AND EGG SAUCE

Used for boiled meats and boiled fish

> 4 *hard-cooked eggs*
> 1 *recipe Mustard Sauce**

Chop eggs and add to Mustard Sauce. Should not be frozen. *Yield:* approximately 3 cups.

ONION SAUCE

Used for liver

> 2 *medium onions, sliced*
> 2 *tablespoons butter or margarine*
> ⅓ *cup dry white wine*
> ¼ *cup vinegar*
> 1 *pint Basic Brown Sauce**

Brown onion in the butter or margarine; add the wine and vinegar and cook until the liquid is reduced to one-half its volume. Add Basic Brown Sauce; heat to desired temperature and serve. Can be frozen. *Yield:* approximately 1 pint.

ORANGE SAUCE FOR ROAST DUCKLING

Used for roast duckling

> *Drippings from Roast Duckling**
> 1 *tablespoon vinegar*
> 1 *tablespoon Red Currant Jelly**
> *Juice 2 oranges*
> *Juice 1 lemon*
> 1 *pint Basic Brown Sauce**
> *Grated rind 1 orange*
> *Grated rind 1 lemon*

Remove the grease dripping from a Roast Duckling and add vinegar, Currant Jelly, the orange and lemon juice, and the Brown Sauce. Cook for 10 minutes on a slow fire. Strain; add the orange and lemon rind and serve. Can be frozen. *Yield:* approximately 1 pint.

OYSTER SAUCE

Used for fish

12 fresh oysters
2 tablespoons butter or margarine
1 pint Fish Velouté*
Juice 1 lemon

Sauté oysters in butter or margarine until they stiffen. Add Velouté and lemon juice. Should not be frozen. *Yield:* approximately 3 cups.

PAPRIKA SAUCE

Used for poultry or veal

2 tablespoons chopped onion
1 teaspoon paprika
4 tablespoons butter or margarine
⅓ cup dry white wine
1 pint Chicken Velouté*

Slowly fry the onions and paprika in 2 tablespoons of butter or margarine; add wine and cook for 5 minutes. Add the Velouté; strain. Place remaining butter or margarine on top of the sauce and gently stir it in to melt it. Can be frozen. *Yield:* approximately 1 pint.

POULETTE SAUCE

Used for poultry

1 cup sliced fresh mushrooms
2 tablespoons butter or margarine

1 pint Chicken Velouté*
4 egg yolks
1 tablespoon chopped chives
¼ cup dry sherry

Cook mushrooms in the butter or margarine for a few minutes, until tender. Add the Velouté and bring to a boil. Remove from fire. Thicken with the egg yolks; add the chives and sherry. Can be frozen before adding sherry. *Yield:* approximately 3 cups.

COLD SAUCES AND DRESSINGS

CAMBRIDGE DRESSING

Used for fish and cold meats

4 hard-cooked egg yolks
1 teaspoon anchovy paste
1 teaspoon capers
1 teaspoon prepared mustard
1 tablespoon tarragon vinegar
½ cup oil
1 tablespoon chopped parsley
Dash Tabasco

Mash the egg yolks and mix with anchovy paste, capers, mustard, and vinegar. Keep stirring and add the oil drop by drop so that the mixture remains thick. The oil may be trickled on as the volume of the mixture increases, but always be careful that not too much oil is added at one time, or the oil will not be incorporated into the dressing. Finish with the parsley and Tabasco. Should not be frozen. *Yield:* approximately 6 servings.

CUMBERLAND SAUCE

Used for cold meats and venison

½ cup Red Currant Jelly*
¼ cup port wine
1 tablespoon chopped blanched shallots or onions
Juice 1 orange
Dash ground ginger
Grated rind 1 orange
Grated rind 1 lemon

Combine the jelly, wine, and shallots or onions in a saucepan and bring to a boil. Add orange juice, ginger, and orange and lemon rinds. Should not be frozen. *Yield:* approximately 6 servings.

AMERICAN STYLE FRENCH DRESSING

Used for salads

2 egg yolks   *⅓ cup vinegar*
1 tablespoon paprika   *1 cup oil*
1 tablespoon sugar

Beat the egg yolks, paprika, sugar, and vinegar thoroughly. Add the oil gradually as directed in the Cambridge Dressing* recipe. Should not be frozen. *Yield:* approximately 1 pint.

CLASSIC FRENCH DRESSING

Used for salads

1½ cups oil   *½ teaspoon ground*
½ cup tarragon vinegar   *pepper*
1 tablespoon salt

Combine ingredients and refrigerate for 2 or 3 days before using. Should not be frozen. *Yield:* approximately 1 pint.

FRUIT SALAD DRESSING

1 cup Mayonnaise*
4 tablespoons unsweetened whipping cream or
   non-dairy whipping cream substitute
⅓ cup juice of fruit for which dressing is intended

Combine all ingredients and serve. Store in refrigerator. Should not be frozen. *Yield:* approximately 1 pint.

GYPSY DRESSING

Used for cold meats and vegetables

½ cup Basic Cream Sauce*
2 tablespoons tarragon vinegar
1 teaspoon salt
½ teaspoon pepper
½ cup oil

Combine the first four ingredients and add the oil as directed in the Cambridge Dressing* recipe. Store in refrigerator. Should not be frozen. *Yield:* approximately 1 cup.

HORSERADISH DRESSING

Used for boiled beef

1 cup sour cream or non-dairy sour cream substitute
2 tablespoons Mayonnaise*
2 tablespoons grated horseradish
Juice 1 lemon

Combine all the ingredients and serve with cold meats. Store in refrigerator. Should not be frozen. *Yield:* approximately 1½ cups.

MAYONNAISE

3 egg yolks at room temperature
3 tablespoons vinegar
Juice ½ lemon
½ tablespoon salt
Dash Tabasco or Cayenne pepper
⅛ teaspoon white pepper
2 cups oil at room temperature
1 tablespoon boiling water

Mix the egg yolks, half the vinegar, the lemon juice and seasonings and beat well. Add the oil a drop at a time, stirring constantly so that each drop of oil is incorporated into the egg mixture. After there is more volume to the egg mixture, the oil can be added in a fine trickle, but care must be taken to keep beating the oil into the thick mixture. If too much oil is present in the bowl, add a little of the vinegar that is left and proceed to stir in a corner of the bowl that has no oil (tip bowl to one side) and while beating add a little of the separated oil at a time until all of it is incorporated in the mixture. Add vinegar if mixture gets too thick. Continue this process until all the oil and vinegar are absorbed. Add boiling water and stir. Refrigerate, but not at a temperature below 35 degrees F. or the Mayonnaise will separate.

The bowl for making the Mayonnaise should be small. If the volume becomes too large for the bowl, then pour the mixture into a little larger bowl. Always use a stainless steel or china bowl.

If your Mayonnaise separates after it has been stored, it can be reconstituted by taking the yolk of 1 egg at room temperature and beating it until thick. Then proceed to add the Mayonnaise (shake it up first) to the egg drop by drop as you would in making the original mixture. Store in refrigerator. Should not be frozen. *Yield:* approximately 3 cups.

EGG-FREE MAYONNAISE

1 tablespoon arrowroot starch, cornstarch or potato
  starch
1 teaspoon salt
3 tablespoons vinegar
1 cup cold water
1 teaspoon prepared mustard
Pinch white pepper
Dash Tabasco
2 cups oil

Dissolve starch, salt, and vinegar in the water. Place in double
boiler and cook until the mixture thickens, stirring quite often; cook
an additional 2 minutes. Remove from fire and let cool to room
temperature. Add mustard, pepper, and Tabasco. Add the oil as
described in the recipe for Mayonnaise*. Store in refrigerator.
Should not be frozen. *Yield:* approximately 3 cups.

MINT SAUCE

Used for roast lamb

3 tablespoons crushed and chopped fresh mint
¼ cup vinegar
½ cup water
2 tablespoons sugar

Combine all ingredients and refrigerate overnight. Can be frozen.
Yield: approximately 1 cup.

REMOULADE SAUCE

Used for fried fish

> 2 cups Mayonnaise*
> 1 teaspoon capers
> 1 teaspoon prepared mustard
> 2 medium-sized sweet pickles, chopped
> 1 tablespoon chopped parsley
> ½ teaspoon dried tarragon

Combine all ingredients and serve. Store in refrigerator. Should not be frozen. *Yield:* approximately 1 pint.

CREAM ROQUEFORT DRESSING

Used for salads

> 1 cup Mayonnaise*
> ½ cup sour cream or non-dairy sour cream substitute
> 2 tablespoons catsup
> 1 garlic clove, minced
> Dash Tabasco
> Juice 1 lemon
> 6 ounces Roquefort cheese, crumbled

Combine all ingredients and serve. Store in refrigerator. Should not be frozen. *Yield:* approximately 1 pint.

SWEDISH SAUCE

Used for cold meats

> 1 cup Mayonnaise*   1 tablespoon horseradish
> ½ cup applesauce   1 tablespoon capers

Mix all ingredients together. Refrigerate until ready to use. Should not be frozen. *Yield:* approximately 1½ cups.

ITALIAN STYLE ROQUEFORT DRESSING

Used for salads

1 pint Classic French Dressing*
1 garlic clove, minced
6 ounces Roquefort cheese, crumbled

Combine all ingredients and serve. Store in refrigerator. Should not be frozen. *Yield:* approximately 2½ cups.

VINAIGRETTE DRESSING

Used for salads or cold meats

6 hard-cooked eggs, chopped
2 medium-sized sweet pickles, chopped
1 tablespoon chopped onion
1 teaspoon capers
1 tablespoon chopped green olives
1 cup oil
¼ cup vinegar
1 teaspoon salt
½ teaspoon pepper
½ teaspoon chopped parsley

Combine all ingredients and serve. Store in refrigerator. Should not be frozen. *Yield:* approximately 1 pint.

TARTAR SAUCE

Used for fish

1 pint Mayonnaise*
4 hard-cooked egg yolks, chopped
1 tablespoon chopped chives
1 tablespoon Worcestershire sauce
Dash Tabasco

Combine all ingredients and serve. Store in refrigerator. Should not be frozen. *Yield:* approximately 1 pint.

CHAPTER 11

FISH AND SHELLFISH

Allergy Key: For those with allergies to meats, these recipes offer alternatives and interest to the diet. For those allergic to the commonly used fish, this chapter includes ideas for new taste treats.

BAKED FISH

2 *pounds salmon steak, swordfish, halibut, red snapper,*
  or fillet of sole
Salt, pepper, paprika to taste
¼ *cup white wine*
Water
3 *tablespoons butter or margarine*

Preheat oven to 375 degrees F. Place fish in greased pan. Add seasonings to fish. Put wine in pan and add water to three-quarters the height of the fish. Dot top with butter or margarine. Cover with waxed paper. Bake about 25 minutes until done. Baste frequently during baking. *Yield:* 4 servings.

BOILED FISH

>   2 *quarts water*
>   1 *medium onion, sliced*
>   1 *stalk celery*
>   1 *tablespoon salt*
>   1 *sprig fresh or pinch dried thyme*
>   1 *sprig parsley*
>   12 *whole peppercorns*
>   2 *pounds fish cleaned: bluefish, halibut, pike, salmon,*
>   *shad roe, red snapper, swordfish, brook trout, or*
>   *tuna*

For cooking shellfish, such as lobster or shrimp, add ¼ cup vinegar.

Put all ingredients into the water and bring to a boil. Reduce heat and simmer until done. The thicker the fish the longer the cooking time. Shrimp take 2–3 minutes; 1-inch-thick fish steaks take about 20 minutes. Serve with Hollandaise Sauce*, Mustard Sauce*, or Butter Sauce*. *Yield:* 4 servings.

BROILED FISH

>   2 *pounds fish, filleted: bass, bluefish, halibut,*
>   *mackerel, oysters, pike, salmon, red snapper, sole,*
>   *swordfish, brook trout, fresh tuna, or whitefish*
>   *Oil*
>   *Salt and pepper*
>   *Flour (any kind) or cornmeal or cracker meal*

Preheat broiler. Dip fish in oil. Season and sprinkle lightly with flour or meal. Place under broiler until done and brown on one side. Turn over and complete cooking. Serve with melted butter, Tartar Sauce*, and lemon quarters. *Yield:* 4 servings.

BROILED LOBSTERS, PRAWNS, AND SCAMPI

2 pounds lobster, prawns, or scampi
4 tablespoons butter or margarine
Salt, pepper, and paprika
Butter or margarine, melted

Preheat broiler. Split fish and season. Dot top with 4 tablespoons butter or margarine. Broil until brown, then finish cooking in 450 degree F. oven for about 25 minutes until done. Serve with melted butter or margarine. *Yield:* 4 servings.

CREAMED FISH

1 teaspoon dry mustard
2 cups Basic Cream Sauce*
1 pound cooked lobster, crab meat, scallops, shrimp,
*   halibut, finnan haddie, oysters, salmon, or any*
*   fish desired*
Salt and pepper to taste
¼ cup dry white wine

Add mustard to Cream Sauce and bring to a boil. Add fish, reduce heat and simmer for 10 minutes. Add salt, pepper, and wine and serve. *Yield:* 3–4 servings.

CREAMED FISH AU GRATIN

Preheat broiler or preheat oven to 450 degrees F. Prepare Creamed Fish*. Place in casserole. Sprinkle top with any kind of cheese desired, bread crumbs, and butter or margarine. Place under broiler or bake in oven until browned.

DEEP FAT FRYING

1 egg
3 tablespoons milk or non-dairy milk substitute
1 pound cleaned fish: frog's legs, oysters, scallops,
    shrimp, smelts, fillet of sole, or any small fish
Salt and pepper to taste
Flour (any kind) for dredging
3 quarts oil at 375 degrees F.

Combine egg and milk or non-dairy milk substitute. Beat well. Dip fish in mixture, season with salt and pepper, and dredge in flour.

Fry in hot oil until done, approximately 3–4 minutes. *Yield:* 3–4 servings.

PAN FRYING

2 pounds fish, filleted: bass, bluefish, frog's legs,
    halibut, mackerel, oysters, pike, salmon, scallops,
    smelts, red snapper, sole, swordfish, brook trout, or
    whitefish
1 cup milk or non-dairy milk substitute, for dipping
Salt and pepper
Flour (any kind) for dredging
4 tablespoons butter or margarine
1 tablespoon lemon juice

Dip fish in milk or non-dairy milk substitute, season, dredge in flour, and place in pan with melted butter or margarine. When fish is nicely browned on one side, turn and complete cooking on the other side, approximately 10–20 minutes in all, depending on thickness of fish. Sprinkle lemon juice over fish and serve. *Yield:* 4 servings.

FRENCH BOUILLABAISE

2 pounds total of perch, pike, snapper, bass, and
   fresh cod
Water
1 medium onion, chopped
Whites 1 leek, minced
1 large fresh tomato, peeled and pressed
1 clove garlic, crushed
1 teaspoon chopped parsley
Pinch saffron
¼ bay leaf
Pinch savory
1 teaspon salt
Dash pepper
2 tablespoons oil
12 clams
12 raw shrimp

Cut fish into strips and put the fish (except codfish) into saucepan. Cover with water and add all remaining ingredients except
codfish, clams, and shrimp. Boil for 10 minutes. Add sliced codfish,
clams, and shrimp and cook another 8 minutes. Serve in deep dish.
Yield: 8 servings.

CLAMS CASINO

12 clams
⅓ cup crumbs of bread or cracker of any kind
4 slices bacon

Preheat broiler. Open clams; place clam on half shell with its
juice on broiler pan. Sprinkle crumbs over top; cover with a slice
of bacon to fit shell. Broil until the bacon is done. *Yield:* 4 servings.

CRAB MEAT BALTIMORE

>2 *shallots, minced*
>2 *tablespoons chopped green pepper*
>2 *tablespoons butter or margarine*
>1 *pound cooked crab meat*
>½ *teaspoon dry mustard*
>*Salt and pepper*
>1 *cup Fish Velouté**
>½ *cup bread crumbs*
>3 *tablespoons butter or margarine, melted*

Preheat broiler. Fry shallots and green pepper in 2 tablespoons butter or margarine for a few minutes. Add crab meat, mustard, salt, pepper, and Velouté and bring to a boil. Pour into a casserole and sprinkle with bread crumbs and melted butter or margarine. Place under broiler until browned. *Yield:* 4 servings.

CODFISH CAKES

>1 *pound salted codfish*
>2 *pounds potatoes, peeled and diced*
>*Salted water*
>8 *tablespoons butter or margarine*
>⅛ *teaspoon white pepper*
>4 *egg yolks*
>*Flour (any kind) for dredging*

Soak codfish in lukewarm water for about 3 hours. Remove from water and take out any small bones. Place fish on a cutting board and cut into shreds.

Cook potatoes in salted boiling water until done. Drain off water and mash the potatoes with 2 tablespoons of butter or margarine and pepper. Add codfish and egg yolks while mixture is still hot. Place in refrigerator until chilled.

When chilled, shape into 8 cakes and dredge in flour. Melt remaining butter or margarine in a shallow pan and fry the codfish cakes on both sides until browned. *Yield:* 4 servings.

CRAB MEAT CAKES

1 cup Basic Cream Sauce*
1 pound cooked crab meat, shredded
6 finely crumbled saltine crackers or all-rye crackers,
    if allergic to wheat
1 tablespoon chopped parsley
½ teaspoon salt
1 teaspoon dry mustard
2 egg yolks
Flour (any kind) for dredging
6 tablespoons butter or margarine

Bring Cream Sauce to a boil. Add crab meat, crackers, parsley, salt, and mustard. Reduce heat and cook over a slow fire for 10 minutes. Remove from fire and add egg yolks. Chill in refrigerator and proceed as for Codfish Cakes*. *Yield:* 4 servings.

LOBSTER NEWBURG

1 pound cooked lobster meat
4 tablespoons butter or margarine
1 teaspoon paprika
½ cup dry sherry
2½ cups 18 per cent cream (coffee cream) or
    non-dairy cream substitute
4 egg yolks
Juice 1 lemon
½ teaspoon salt
Dash Cayenne pepper or Tabasco

Cut lobster meat in half-inch slices. Melt butter or margarine in heavy skillet. Add lobster. Sprinkle with paprika. Cook until lobster meat acquires a fine reddish color; add sherry and reduce the liquid almost entirely.

Add 2 cups cream or non-dairy cream substitute (reserve ½ cup for blending with egg yolks). Cook at a fast boil until sauce is reduced to about two-thirds of its volume. Mix remaining cream or non-dairy cream substitute with the egg yolks, lemon juice, salt, and Cayenne pepper or Tabasco sauce; stir in gently on low heat until mixture has thickened. (Be careful not to boil.) Serve with rice or toast in lukewarm dish. *Yield:* 4 servings.

LOBSTER THERMIDOR

> 2 *pounds fresh live lobster*
> *Water*
> 2 *shallots, chopped*
> 4 *large mushrooms, minced*
> 3 *tablespoons butter or margarine*
> ½ *teaspoon dry mustard*
> 2 *tablespoons white wine*
> ½ *cup Fish Velouté**
> *Salt and pepper to taste*
> ¾ *cup bread crumbs (from any kind of bread)*
> 3 *tablespoons butter or margarine, melted*

Preheat broiler. Boil lobster for 20 minutes in water to cover. Split and remove meat from body and claws. Save the shells. Dice meat into small pieces. Fry shallots and mushrooms in butter or margarine until mushrooms are cooked. Add mustard, wine, and Fish Velouté and bring to a boil. Add salt and pepper and lobster meat. Stuff the lobster shells with the mixture and top with bread crumbs and melted butter. Broil until golden brown. *Yield:* 4 servings.

LOBSTER SALAD

6 ounces cooked lobster meat
2 stalks celery, diced
½ cup cocktail sauce or Mayonnaise*
Lettuce
2 fresh tomatoes, quartered
2 hard-cooked eggs, sliced
8 olives

Mix lobster, celery, and cocktail sauce or Mayonnaise. Place on lettuce bed and use remaining ingredients for garnish. *Yield:* 4 servings.

BROILED SCAMPI AND DANISH LOBSTER TAILS

8 scampi or Danish lobster tails
Garlic Butter*
Salt

Preheat broiler. Split, devein, and wash scampi or lobster tails. Place in baking dish, spread top with Garlic Butter. Add a dash of salt to each one. Place under broiler for 10 minutes. *Yield:* 4 servings.

To make Garlic Butter combine 1 clove garlic, minced, and 2 tablespoons soft butter or margarine.

SHRIMP NEWBURG

Proceed as for Lobster Newburg*, but substitute 1 pound shrimp for lobster.

SHRIMP SPANISH STYLE

1 medium onion, minced
2 celery stalks, minced
4 large mushrooms
1 medium green pepper, chopped
4 tablespoons butter or margarine
½ bay leaf
Salt and pepper
Pinch saffron
4 medium fresh tomatoes, peeled and deseeded
24 cooked shrimp
1 teaspoon arrowroot starch, cornstarch, or potato
  starch diluted in ¼ cup water

Fry onion, celery, mushrooms, and green pepper in butter or margarine for 5 minutes. Add bay leaf, salt, pepper, saffron, and tomatoes and cook until vegetables are done. Add shrimp and starch. Bring to a boil. Serve with rice. *Yield:* 4 servings.

SHRIMP VICTORIA

2 cups whole mushrooms
¼ cup butter or margarine
1 pound uncooked shrimp
2 tablespoons minced onion
1 tablespoon wheat flour or 2 teaspoons cornstarch
  diluted in 2 teaspoons water
½ teaspoon salt
Dash freshly ground pepper
½ pint sour cream or non-dairy sour cream substitute
¼ cup sherry

Preheat oven to 350 degrees F. Sauté mushrooms in half the butter or margarine until done; set aside. Sauté shrimp and onion in remaining butter or margarine until shrimp is pink (about 3 minutes). Add mushrooms and cook an additional 5 minutes; add more butter or margarine if necessary. Sprinkle with flour or diluted cornstarch, salt and pepper. Cook gently until hot. At this point the mixture can be cooled and refrigerated, if you wish to make it ahead of time. When ready to reheat, put in casserole and reheat in oven at 350 degrees F. until hot; reheat only enough so that the casserole is heated through. Add the sour cream or non-dairy sour cream substitute (at room temperature) and sherry just before serving. Serve at once. *Yield:* 4 servings.

RED SNAPPER DUCALE

4 six-ounce pieces filleted and skinned red snapper
Salt and pepper
2 shallots, sliced
4 large mushrooms, sliced
4 tablespoons butter or margarine
2 medium fresh tomatoes, peeled, deseeded, and mashed
½ cup water
¼ cup dry white wine
1 egg yolk
Juice ½ lemon
¼ cup 18 per cent cream (coffee cream) or non-dairy cream substitute

Preheat oven to 375 degrees F. Place fish in buttered casserole. Add all ingredients except egg yolk, lemon juice, and cream or non-dairy cream substitute. Cover with waxed paper. Bake for 25 minutes. Remove fish and cook liquid on stove until it is reduced to one-half its volume. Add egg yolk, lemon juice, and cream or non-dairy cream substitute. Stir. Pour over fish and serve. *Yield:* 4 servings.

RED SNAPPER MIRABEAU

Proceed as for Red Snapper Ducale* but omit tomatoes and add 6 small cooked artichoke hearts and 4 strips of anchovy fillets before serving.

FILLET OF SOLE VERONIQUE

> *Salt and Pepper*
> *4 six-ounce fillets of sole*
> *1 shallot, chopped*
> *1 teaspoon chopped parsley*
> *Juice 1 lemon*
> *¼ cup white wine*
> *1 egg yolk*
> *¼ cup 18 per cent cream (coffee cream) or non-dairy*
>   *cream substitute*
> *1 tablespoon butter or margarine*
> *Seedless grapes for garnish*

Preheat oven to 350 degrees F. Season and put fish fillets together. Place in greased casserole. Add shallot, parsley, lemon juice, and wine. Bake for 20 minutes. Remove fish to a warm plate. Bring liquid to a boil on the stove. Add egg yolk, cream, or non-dairy cream substitute and butter or margarine. Pour over fish. Garnish with grapes. *Yield:* 4 servings.

FILLET OF SOLE NEWBURG

Bake fillet of sole as for Veronique*, but make sauce as in Lobster Newburg*, and cover fish with it. Garnish with toast points.

CHAPTER 12

MEAT, POULTRY, AND GAME

Allergy Key: The meat course is the staple of every full meal. This chapter presents a variety of meats so that those allergic to chicken, for example, will be able to choose from a large list of substitution ideas. Where thickeners are needed, any of the thickening agents listed in Chapter I can be used. The herb list in Chapter I will assist you in selecting permissible seasonings.

Sausage recipes have been included for those who are concerned about the contents of commercial sausages (which may contain wheat, soybean, or milk fillers).

PRINCIPAL METHODS OF COOKING MEAT

ROASTING:

Cooking with dry heat. The roasting pan should be heavy and just large enough for the meat. No liquid should be added while cooking, but the meat should be basted frequently with its own juices. Meats best suited for roasting are: *beef:* tenderloin, rump roast, standing rib, and sirloin; *lamb:* rack, loin, and leg; *pork:* rib, loin, and fresh ham; *poultry and game; veal:* leg, loin, and shoulder.

TIMETABLE FOR ROASTING MEATS

All weights are for fully trimmed meat. All oven temperatures are 325 degrees F. Season with salt and pepper to taste. Use meat thermometer to permit adjustment for variation in oven efficiency and quantity of food being roasted in the same oven.

Standing Rib of Beef	6–8 pounds	2–2½	hours for rare
		2½–3	hours for medium
		3½–4	hours for well done
Roast Sirloin of Beef	3 pounds (larger roasts will not take much longer)	1–1¼	hours for rare
		1¾	hours for medium
		2 hours for well done	
Veal Leg	5–8 pounds	2½–3½ hours	
Veal Loin	5 pounds	3 hours	
Rolled Veal Shoulder	3–5 pounds	3½ hours	
Leg of Lamb	6 pounds	3 hours	
Rolled Lamb Shoulder	3–5 pounds	2½–3 hours	
Pork Loin	3–5 pounds	1½–3 hours	
Pork Shoulder	5–8 pounds	3½–5 hours	
Whole Fresh Ham	10–14 pounds	5½–7 hours	
Half Fresh Ham	5–7 pounds	2½–3½ hours	

BRAISING:

Cooking with moisture. Meat is browned on all sides in clarified butter or fat and placed in another pan on a bed of 1 onion, 2 celery stalks, 1 medium carrot, diced, 1 bay leaf, and 1 sprig fresh or pinch dried thyme. Cook covered on top of the stove over low heat until vegetables are slightly browned. Add 4 fresh tomatoes,

diced, season with salt and pepper to taste. Add enough Beef Stock*
or water to cover and place in a 350 degree F. oven until done.
Remove meat to a warm platter, thicken gravy with 2–3 tablespoons
of starch (corn, arrowroot, or potato) diluted in a small amount of
cold water. Strain and serve with meat.

Less expensive cuts of good quality meats are used for braising.
Game is also braised.

BROILING:

Or grilling. Use high heat for red meats such as beef, mutton,
lamb, or liver. They should be seared quickly to seal in the juices.
Smaller cuts of white meat such as pork, veal, poultry, sweetbreads,
brains, etc., are first broiled at high heat for a few minutes and
then the heat is reduced to a moderate temperature for the remaining cooking time.

PAN FRYING:

Cooking with a minimum of fat in a heavy skillet. All pan frying
is done over medium heat with a minimum of fat. Red meats such
as beef, lamb, mutton, and liver are fried without dredging in flour,
but veal, pork, poultry, sweetbreads, brains, and other variety meats
are dredged in flour before frying. When cooking is completed, remove meat, discard fat, and add wine or Beef Stock* to the skillet;
swill to absorb the remaining flavors and use as a sauce for the
meat.

DEEP FAT FRYING:

The quantity of fat should be 7 times the quantity of the food
to be fried. Foods are either breaded or dipped in a batter before
frying. Red meats should be fried at moderate heat. Variety meats
such as sweetbreads and precooked meats such as croquettes are
fried at high heat.

POACHING:

Cooking without boiling. Place meat in water and bring water to the boiling point. Skim off impurities. Add salt, pepper, and herbs. Continue cooking at a slow simmer to prevent excessive evaporation of the liquid and to prevent breaking the skin of fowl and the clouding of soup stocks. There is no advantage in boiling meat at high heat because the cooking time will not be shortened thereby.

ROAST BEEF TENDERLOIN

4-pound (approximately) full beef tenderloin (fully trimmed)
Suet from tenderloin
Salt and pepper to taste

Preheat oven to 425 degrees F. Place beef tenderloin on broiler pan; cover the top with suet. Add salt and pepper. Use a meat thermometer.

Roast for 30 minutes at 425 degrees F.; turn temperature down to 350 degrees F. and roast for another 30 minutes for medium rare, or longer for better done meat. *Yield:* approximately 8–10 servings.

This is very good served with Mushroom Sauce I or II*.

BRAISED FRESH BRISKET OF BEEF

4 pound brisket of beef, well trimmed
Salt and pepper to taste
3 medium fresh tomatoes, sliced
1 medium onion, sliced
1 carrot, sliced
2 celery stalks
1 whole bay leaf
2 sprigs fresh or 2 pinches dried thyme
1 quart water

Preheat oven to 325 degrees F. Rub the meat with salt and pepper and place in greased roasting pan. Bake for 1 hour. Add the vegetables and herbs and bake until vegetables are golden brown. Add water and continue baking. Baste frequently. Bake about 3 hours total or until meat is tender. Remove meat and slice against the grain, about ¼-inch-thick slices. Strain gravy and serve with meat. *Yield:* approximately 8–10 servings.

FLEMISH CARBONADES

> *2 pounds boneless beef chuck, sliced thin*
> *Flour for dredging (any kind)*
> *Fat for browning meat*
> *1 pound onions, sliced*
> *1 teaspoon salt*
> *⅛ teaspoon pepper*
> *1 sprig fresh or pinch dried thyme*
> *½ bay leaf*
> *2 tablespoons brown sugar*
> *12 ounces dark beer*
> *6 tablespoons flour (any kind)*
> *4 tablespoons melted butter or margarine*

Dredge beef slices in flour and brown in fat on both sides in a heavy saucepan. Remove the meat and fry the onion slices until lightly colored. Return meat to pan and add seasonings, herbs, sugar, and beer. Simmer covered about 1½ hours or until meat is tender. Remove meat. Mix flour and melted butter or margarine. Add to gravy, stir, and cook for 15 minutes. Serve gravy over meat. *Yield:* approximately 6 servings.

BEEF SHORT RIBS

3 pounds trimmed beef short ribs
1–2 tablespoons butter, margarine, or oil
1 medium onion, chopped
2 celery stalks
3 carrots, cut in half
1 sprig thyme or ½ teaspoon dried thyme
¼ bay leaf
1½ tablespoons salt
Pepper to taste
½ cup tomato paste or 4 fresh tomatoes, chopped
Hot water to cover
2–3 tablespoons flour, cornstarch, arrowroot, or
  potato starch

Brown the meat in the fat; add the onion, celery, carrots, thyme, bay leaf, salt, pepper, tomato paste or tomatoes, and hot water to cover. Cook over low heat for 2–3 hours until the meat is tender. Remove the meat and vegetables and add the flour or starch to the liquid until it is the desired thickness. Return the meat and vegetables to the liquid and serve. *Yield:* 4 servings.

This recipe is even better if cooked a few hours or a day ahead of time. Refrigerate when cool and when ready to reheat, first heat on top of the stove until the gravy bubbles; then heat in oven at 350 degrees F. until hot throughout.

BEEF SHISH KABOB

1 pound beef tenderloin or choice top sirloin butt
  cut into 1-inch cubes
½ cup red wine (any kind)
½ cup oil
3 tablespoons chopped onion
1 garlic clove, minced

2 teaspoons rosemary
1 teaspoon peppercorns
4 strips bacon
1 cup whole mushrooms
1 cup small white onions
½ cup green pepper cubes
10 small whole fresh tomatoes

Place a layer of meat in a large bowl. Then sprinkle some of the wine, oil, and seasonings on top of the meat. Then place another layer of meat and another layer of wine, oil, and seasonings on top until all the ingredients are used up. Refrigerate for at least 24 hours. Turn the mixture in the bowl every 3 or 4 hours.

Place on skewers alternately with bacon, mushrooms, small white onions (par-boiled), cubes of green pepper (boiled for about 5 minutes), and small whole fresh tomatoes.

Cook over a charcoal fire or under broiler until done. *Yield:* approximately 3–4 servings.

HUNGARIAN BEEF GOULASH

2 pounds boneless beef chuck cut into 1-inch cubes
2 tablespoons flour (any kind)
2 tablespoons butter, margarine, or oil
1 tablespoon salt
¼ teaspoon pepper
1 tablespoon paprika
1 medium onion, chopped fine
Water to cover meat
½ cup sour cream or non-dairy sour cream substitute
  at room temperature

Dredge beef cubes in flour and brown in fat in a heavy saucepan. Add seasonings, onions, and water. Stir well. Bring water to a boil; cover and simmer for 2 hours or until meat is tender. Add sour cream or non-dairy sour cream substitute and serve. *Yield:* approximately 4 servings.

POT ROAST OF BEEF

> *3 pound boneless rump roast*
> *2 tablespoons fat, any kind (optional)*
> *1 medium onion, sliced*
> *1 carrot, sliced*
> *2 celery stalks, sliced*
> *½ bay leaf*
> *2 sprigs fresh or 2 pinches dried thyme*
> *2 medium fresh tomatoes, peeled and diced*
> *1 tablespoon salt*
> *⅛ teaspoon pepper*
> *1 quart water*
> *2 tablespoons melted butter or margarine*
> *2 tablespoons flour (any kind)*

Brown meat on all sides in a heavy saucepan. If the meat does not have any fat cover, add fat ingredients for browning. Add onion, carrot, celery, bay leaf, and thyme and cook until the vegetables are lightly colored. Add tomatoes, seasonings, and water. Cover and simmer for about 2 hours or until meat is done. Remove meat. Mix melted butter or margarine and flour and add to gravy in the saucepan. Cook gravy for 15 minutes. Strain and serve with the meat. *Yield:* approximately 6 servings.

VEAL STEW

> *3 pounds veal shoulder cut into 1-inch cubes*
> *2 small garlic cloves, minced*
> *2 tablespoons shortening*
> *2 tablespoons flour or starch (any kind), diluted in 2 tablespoons water*
> *3 tablespoons tomato paste or 6 fresh tomatoes, peeled and deseeded*
> *1 tablespoon salt*
> *Pepper to taste*

2–3 cups boiling water, approximately
2 bay leaves
Pinch dried parsley
Pinch thyme
Pinch marjoram
2 pounds potatoes
1 pound small white onions
1 pound carrots
1 pound fresh peas

Brown the veal and garlic in the shortening; mix in the flour or diluted starch thoroughly; add the tomato paste, salt, and pepper, and enough boiling water to cover. Simmer, covered, for 1 hour, then add all the remaining ingredients except the peas. Simmer 1 more hour or until the meat is tender. Remove from fire and add the peas, stirring them in thoroughly. *Yield:* 6–8 servings.

This recipe is best if made a few hours or a day ahead of time. Refrigerate when cool and, when ready to reheat, first heat on top of the stove until the liquid bubbles; then heat in oven at 350 degrees F. until hot throughout.

STUFFED VEAL SCROLLS

8 three-ounce boneless veal cutlets, sliced thin
Salt and pepper to taste
½ pound Meat Loaf* uncooked
Flour for dredging (any kind)
3 tablespoons butter or margarine
2 cups sliced mushrooms
1 pint cream or non-dairy cream substitute or
Brown Sauce*

Preheat oven to 325 degrees F. Pound veal cutlets on a flat surface to a size approximately 2 inches by 4 inches. Sprinkle lightly with salt and pepper. Divide Meat Loaf preparation into eight equal portions. Place Meat Loaf on veal cutlets; roll cutlets; fasten with toothpick and dredge in flour. Brown scrolls in butter or margarine over moderate fire. Add sliced mushrooms and cook for 10 minutes. Add cream or non-dairy cream substitute or Brown Sauce and bake for 25 minutes. *Yield:* 4–6 servings.

STUFFED VEAL BREAST

> 1 *whole 4-pound boneless veal breast*
> 1 *pound Meat Loaf*, uncooked*
> 1 *cup boiled rice*
> 1 *tablespoon chopped chives*
> *Salt and pepper to taste*
> 2 *cups Beef or Veal Stock**

Preheat oven to 300 degrees F. Take a small knife and make as large an opening as possible in the veal breast (start on the thick end of the breast). Be careful not to break the skin while cutting. Combine the Meat Loaf, rice, and chives and mix thoroughly. Stuff this mixture into the veal breast and close the open end with heavy toothpicks. Rub the breast with salt and pepper. Place in greased roasting pan and put in oven. When the breast is brown, add the stock and use for basting during the baking time. Total baking time is about 3 hours or until the meat is tender. *Yield:* 8 servings.

VEAL SAUTE VALENCIENNES

> 2 *pounds boneless veal steak*
> 1 *teaspoon salt*
> ⅛ *teaspoon pepper*
> 2 *tablespoons flour (any kind)*
> 4 *tablespoons butter or margarine*
> 4 *green onions, sliced*
> 2 *cups sliced fresh mushrooms*
> ½ *cup dry white wine*
> 2 *cups 18 per cent cream (coffee cream) or non-dairy cream substitute*

Cut veal in 1-inch strips; season and dredge in flour. Sauté in butter or margarine over low heat until brown. Add green onions and mushrooms; let simmer with meat until soft. Add wine and cream or non-dairy cream substitute. Cook over moderate heat for about 35 minutes or until veal is tender. Serve in Rice Pilaff* ring. *Yield:* approximately 4 servings.

BRAISED SHOULDER LAMB CHOPS CHAMPVALLON

> 6 *eight-ounce shoulder lamb chops*
> 1 *teaspoon salt*
> ⅛ *teaspoon pepper*
> *Fat, any kind desired, for browning (optional)*
> 3 *medium onions, thinly sliced*
> 2 *cups water*
> 1 *clove garlic, minced*
> 2 *cups sliced fresh mushrooms*
> 1 *small bay leaf*
> *Pinch powdered thyme*
> 6 *medium potatoes, peeled and thinly sliced*

Preheat oven to 350 degrees F. Season lamb chops with salt and pepper; brown slowly in heavy skillet. There should be enough fat on the meat for browning; if not, add fat, remove chops to earthenware or Pyrex dish. Use same skillet and remaining fat to fry onions to a golden color; add water; simmer for a few minutes and pour over lamb chops. Add garlic, mushrooms, bay leaf, and thyme. Bring to a boil, then bake in the oven for 30 minutes. Add potatoes and cook 20 minutes longer, basting all the while.

When chops are cooked, moisture should be reduced to almost 1 cup of liquid. *Yield:* approximately 6 servings.

BOILED LAMB SHOULDER, CAPER SAUCE

> 1 whole 4-pound boneless lamb shoulder, rolled and
>   tied
> Salted water to cover
> 6 medium turnips, sliced
> 6 medium carrots, sliced
> 2 small white onions, sliced
> 2 cloves garlic, minced
> 2 sprigs fresh or 2 pinches dried thyme
> 1 small bay leaf
> Caper Sauce*

Place meat and salted water in a pot just large enough to hold them. Simmer 1½ hours; add vegetables and herbs and cook for another half hour. Serve with Caper Sauce*. *Yield:* approximately 8 servings.

ROAST LEG OF SPRING LAMB, MINT SAUCE

> 6-pound leg of lamb
> 1 garlic clove
> Salt and pepper to taste
> 1 carrot, chopped
> 1 medium onion, chopped
> 1 stalk celery, chopped
> ½ bay leaf
> 1 sprig fresh or pinch dried thyme
> 1 quart Beef Stock*
> Mint Sauce*

Preheat oven to 350 degrees F. Remove excess fat, shank, and aitch (H) bone of lamb, leaving only the center bone. Insert garlic

clove in shank and tie in place. Rub with salt and pepper. Place
in roasting pan. Add vegetables and herbs. Roast in oven, allowing
30 minutes per pound. When done, remove lamb to a warm platter.
Remove fat drippings from pan. Add Beef Stock to the vegetables
and gravy. Simmer 10 minutes; strain and serve with lamb. Serve
with Mint Sauce*. *Yield:* approximately 8 servings.

LAMB SHISH KABOB

1 pound lamb leg or shoulder cut into 1-inch cubes
2 bay leaves
1 teaspoon minced garlic
1 teaspoon allspice
¼ cup oil
½ cup white wine
4 strips bacon
1 cup whole mushrooms
1 cup small white onions
½ cup green pepper cubes
10 small whole fresh tomatoes

Place a layer of meat in a large bowl. Then sprinkle some of
the seasonings, oil, and wine on top of the meat. Then place another
layer of meat and another layer of seasonings, oil, and wine on
top until all the ingredients are used up. Refrigerate for at least
24 hours. Turn the mixture in the bowl every 3 or 4 hours.

Place on skewers alternately with bacon, mushrooms, small white
onions (par-boiled), cubes of green pepper (boiled for about 5 minutes), and small whole fresh tomatoes.

Cook over a charcoal fire or under broiler until done. *Yield:* approximately 3–4 servings.

BAKED HAM

5-pound smoked ham
Whole cloves
2 teaspoons dry mustard
2 tablespoons cider vinegar
¾ cup maple syrup
1 8¼-ounce can pineapple slices and juice
Maraschino cherries and some juice

Preheat oven to 350 degrees F. With a knife, cut a diamond pattern across the top of the ham. Insert cloves where the cut lines intersect. Combine the dry mustard, vinegar, maple syrup, pineapple juice, and some of the maraschino cherry juice. Decorate the top of the ham with pineapple slices and cherries held down with toothpicks. Baste with the liquid. Bake until done, basting every half hour. The amount of cooking time will depend on how fully cooked a ham you are using. *Yield:* approximately 10 servings.

BAKED COUNTRY HAM

10–12-pound country smoked ham
Cold water
½ pound hay or dried grass
1½ cups brown sugar
2 tablespoons dry mustard

Soak ham in cold water to cover for 20 minutes. Drain and remove pelvic bone. Place in pot and cover with cold water. Add the hay and simmer uncovered for 20 minutes per pound.

Preheat oven to 350 degrees F. Remove skin; place in roasting pan. Score top and spread on the brown sugar and dry mustard. Bake for 1 hour. *Yield:* allow ½ pound per person.

DUTCH STYLE PORK CHOPS

Salt and pepper to taste
4 thick pork chops (approximately 8 ounces each)
4 tablespoons butter or margarine
2 large eating apples, peeled and sliced
4 tablespoons brown sugar
½ cup dry white wine

Season pork chops. Sauté in the butter or margarine until browned. Place sliced apples in bottom of fireproof casserole. Place pork chops over apples. Add sugar and wine and simmer for 1 hour or until chops are tender. *Yield:* 4 servings.

SPARE RIBS

3–4 pounds pork spare ribs, cut in pieces
1 lemon, sliced
1 large onion, sliced
1 cup catsup
⅓ cup Worcestershire sauce
1 teaspoon chili powder
1 teaspoon salt
2 dashes Tabasco
2 cups water
Honey (optional)

Preheat oven at 450 degrees F. Put ribs in shallow roasting pan with meat side up. Put slice of lemon and slice of onion on top of each piece. Roast at 450 degrees F. for 30 minutes. Combine the other ingredients and pour over the ribs. Turn oven down to 350 degrees F. for 1 hour. Baste frequently with the drippings. Add water if the sauce gets too thick. *Yield:* 3–4 servings.

MEAT LOAF

8 slices bread (any kind)
1 cup milk or non-dairy milk substitute
1 pound beef, ground
½ pound pork, ground
½ pound veal, ground
3 eggs
1 medium onion, chopped
1 tablespoon salt
1 teaspoon freshly ground black pepper
1 sprig fresh or pinch dried thyme
1 bay leaf, chopped
1 tablespoon chopped parsley

Preheat oven to 325 degrees F. Soften the bread in the milk or non-dairy milk substitute. Combine all the ingredients and mix well by hand. Shape into an oblong loaf and place in a greased baking pan. Place in oven. When the loaf has formed a brown crust, add a small amount of water to the pan and use for basting while baking. Bake for approximately 45 minutes. *Yield:* 8 servings.

MEAT BALLS

Proceed as for Meat Loaf* and shape into 1-inch balls. Fry in 3 tablespoons butter or margarine for about 10 minutes over a moderate fire. *Yield:* 6–8 servings.

SHERRIED LAMB KIDNEY SAUTE

6 lamb kidneys
Salt and pepper to taste
3 tablespoons oil
½ cup Brown Sauce*
3 tablespoons dry sherry

Split kidneys lengthwise and remove white membrane from the center. Cut into ¼-inch slices. Season with salt and pepper. Fry in hot oil for about 5 minutes. Add Brown Sauce and bring to a boil. Add sherry and serve. *Yield:* 4 servings.

SAUTEED CHICKEN LIVERS

1 pound chicken livers
3 tablespoons butter or margarine
1 medium onion, chopped
1 sprig fresh or pinch dried thyme
⅛ bay leaf
1 teaspoon salt
Pinch pepper
2 tablespoons dry sherry

Brown livers in butter or margarine; add remaining ingredients and cook until livers are cooked through. Do not overcook or the livers will toughen. *Yield:* 3–4 servings.

PAN FRIED LIVER VIZCAYA

Salt and pepper
8 slices liver, calf or baby beef
Flour (any kind) for dredging
4 tablespoons butter or margarine
¼ cup chopped scallions
Juice 2 lemons
½ cup water
1 medium-sized avocado, peeled and sliced
2 medium-sized oranges, peeled and sliced

Dredge seasoned liver in flour. Sauté in butter or margarine until brown on both sides. Do not overcook. Remove liver to warm plates. In skillet in which liver was cooked, sauté scallions until tender without browning. Add lemon juice and water. Simmer until juices in skillet are dissolved. Dish sauce over liver and garnish top with avocado and orange slices. *Yield:* 4–6 servings.

PRECOOKING OF SWEETBREADS

> *2 pounds sweetbreads*
> *Water to cover*
> *2 quarts cold water*
> *1 tablespoon salt*
> *12 peppercorns*
> *1 celery stalk*
> *1 medium onion, sliced*
> *1 bay leaf*
> *¼ cup white vinegar*
> *1 sprig fresh or pinch dried thyme*

Combine all ingredients except the sweetbreads. Simmer for 20 minutes. In the meantime, place the sweetbreads (which should be free from bloodstains) in cold water and soak for a half hour. Add the sweetbreads to the simmering stock and simmer for 15 minutes. Drain the sweetbreads; cool and refrigerate until ready for use.

CREAMED SWEETBREADS

> *1 pound Precooked Sweetbreads*, diced*
> *2 cups Basic Cream Sauce**
> *2 cups sliced mushrooms, cooked in 3 tablespoons*
> * butter or margarine*
> *⅛ cup dry sherry*

Combine sweetbreads, Cream Sauce, and mushrooms and heat thoroughly, either in the oven (preheated to 350 degrees F.) or on top of the stove over a moderate fire. Remove from heat and stir in sherry. Serve immediately on toast or patty shells. *Yield:* 6–8 servings.

BROILED SWEETBREADS

2 pounds Precooked Sweetbreads*
Salt and pepper to taste
Oil (any kind except olive oil) for dredging

Split the sweetbreads and season with salt and pepper. Dredge in oil. Place under broiler until browned. *Yield:* 4 servings.

SAUTEED SWEETBREADS

2 pounds Precooked Sweetbreads*
Salt and pepper to taste
Milk or non-dairy milk substitute for dredging
Flour (any kind) for dredging
4 tablespoons butter or margarine for frying

Split the sweetbreads. Season with salt and pepper. Dredge first in milk or non-dairy milk substitute, then in flour. Fry in butter or margarine until browned. *Yield:* 4 servings.

BOILED FRESH BEEF TONGUE

1 four–five-pound steer beef tongue, trimmed
1 medium onion, chopped
1 bay leaf
1 whole carrot
1 lemon, quartered
2 celery stalks
1 tablespoon salt
1 teaspoon whole peppercorns

Wash tongue. Place in 6-quart-size casserole. Add all other ingredients. Simmer for about 2 hours, or until tender. Let cool in cooking liquid; remove skin; serve hot or cold. *Yield:* 8–10 servings.

SMOKED MEATS OR BEEF TONGUES

Proceed as for Boiled Fresh Beef Tongue*. But omit salt.

PICKLED MEATS

Cover with cold water; bring to a boil and cook for 15 minutes. Drain, again cover with cold water, and cook until done. Let cool in cooking liquid. Serve hot or cold.

PICKLING BRINE FOR MEATS

   5 quarts water
   5½ pounds coarse or Kosher salt
   1 potato, peeled
   8 ounces saltpeter (available at drugstores)
   1½ cups whole allspice
   ½ cup brown sugar

Bring water and salt to a boil. Place potato in liquid. If potato floats, add water until it begins to sink. If potato should sink immediately, reduce liquid until it is able to float. Add saltpeter, allspice, and sugar. Allow to cool and place in stone or enamel container. Store in cool place. Meats should be pricked all over with large needle before placing in brine and be weighted down to prevent from rising to top. Meats up to 4 pounds need about 6 days in brine.

Meats for pickling: Fairly flat pieces of meat that are not too thick are best for home pickling because the brine solution can penetrate more readily. For commercial operations, the brine is pumped into the meat for uniform curing, so that even thick pieces of meat can be pickled successfully. Any meat can be cured. Some suggestions are steer or calf tongues (all throat cartilage should be removed), briskets of beef with the deckle off, beef rounds, beef rumps, beef chucks, fresh ham or pork butts.

Sausage Note: Sausage casings can be purchased in specialty or nationality food stores.

PORK SAUSAGE

1 medium onion, diced
1 pound fresh bacon fat
¼ pound calf liver, diced
1 pound fresh lean pork, diced
4 eggs
1 cup boiled milk or non-dairy milk substitute that has been cooled
1 tablespoon salt
1 teaspoon white pepper
½ teaspoon ground nutmeg
8 to 10 feet sausage casing
String for tying

Fry the onion in a small amount of the bacon fat until just before the onion takes on color. Add the liver and fry until liver stiffens. Remove from fire and add remainder of bacon fat and the pork. Put through the fine blade of meat grinder. Add the eggs one at a time and mix thoroughly. Gradually add milk or non-dairy milk substitute and seasonings and blend well. Tie one end of sausage casing with string and fill from the other end. Do not pack the mixture in too tight to allow for some expansion while cooking. Tie the sausage in 6-inch lengths. Place sausage in hot water that is kept just below the boiling point, for 15 minutes. Remove sausage from water; cool and refrigerate. To serve, broil at moderate temperature for about 10 minutes. *Yield:* 6–8 servings.

CHICKEN AND HAM SAUSAGE

1 medium onion, diced
1 small bay leaf
1 sprig fresh or pinch dried thyme
¾ pound fresh bacon fat
1 pound boneless and skinless chicken, diced
1 tablespoon salt
1 teaspoon white pepper
4 eggs
1½ cups boiled milk or non-dairy milk substitute
   that has been cooled
½ pound baked ham, finely diced
8 to 10 feet sausage casing
String for tying

Fry the onion, bay leaf, and thyme in a small amount of the bacon fat until just before the onion takes on color. Remove from fire. Add the chicken, remainder of bacon fat, and seasonings. Put through the fine blade of meat grinder. Add the eggs one at a time and mix thoroughly. Gradually add milk or non-dairy milk substitute, blending completely. Add ham and stuff into sausage casing in 6-inch lengths. Complete cooking as described in Pork Sausage*. *Yield:* 6 servings.

YORKSHIRE SAUSAGE

1 medium onion, diced
1 small bay leaf
1 sprig fresh or pinch dried thyme
1 pound fresh bacon fat
1 cup fresh bread crumbs (from any kind of bread)
1 cup boiled cream or non-dairy cream substitute
   that has been cooled
1 tablespoon salt

1 tablespoon sugar
1 pound fresh lean pork, diced
3 eggs
½ cup raisins, parboiled
8 to 10 feet sausage casing
String for tying

Fry the onion, bay leaf, and thyme in a small amount of the bacon fat until just before the onion takes on color. Remove from fire. Moisten the bread crumbs with the cream or non-dairy cream substitute. Add salt and sugar to the bread crumb-cream mixture and add to the onion mixture. Add pork and remainder of bacon fat and put through fine blade of a meat grinder. Add eggs one at a time, mixing thoroughly. Mix in raisins. Stuff into sausage casing in 6-inch lengths. Complete cooking as described in Pork Sausage*. *Yield:* 6–8 servings.

COUNTRY STYLE PATE

1 large onion, chopped
1 medium bay leaf
1 sprig fresh or pinch dried thyme
1 pound fresh bacon fat
1 pound calf liver, diced
1 pound fresh lean pork, diced
1 pound fresh veal, diced
2 tablespoons salt
1 teaspoon freshly ground pepper
5 eggs
½ cup dry Madeira wine
10–12 bacon strips

Preheat oven to 350 degrees F. Fry onion, bay leaf, and thyme in a small amount of the bacon fat until just before the onion takes on color. Add calf liver and cook until liver stiffens. Remove from fire. Add pork, veal, and remainder of bacon fat. Put through medium blade of meat grinder. Add seasonings, eggs, and Madeira, and blend well. Line a 2-quart casserole with the bacon. Add meat mixture. Place in pan of hot water and bake for 1 hour. Serve hot or cold as main course or use in sandwiches. *Yield:* as a main course, serves 12.

MARINADES

Marinades are the original meat preservers and tenderizers. The original function of a marinade was the softening of the fibers and preservation of meat. What the meat gains in tenderness it loses in its natural flavor. Usually, the less tender cuts are used for marinating.

Cooked marinades are used for any red meats, even the tender cuts. Refrigerate meat while marinating. Turn meat over every few hours if marinating for a short time or turn at least twice daily when marinating for a few days. Marinating timing varies from a few hours for steaks or chops up to three days for larger cuts such as saddle or legs of mutton.

Uncooked marinades are used for any less tender red meats and also for such meats as mutton, moose, elk, venison, and bear meat. Rub meat with salt and pepper and place in a container just large enough to hold it. Add marinade; cover and keep in a cool place or refrigerate. Turn meat at least twice daily. Marinate meat from several hours up to three days depending on the toughness of the meat.

COOKED MARINADE FOR MEATS AND VENISON

  ¼ *cup oil*
  1 medium carrot, diced
  1 medium onion, diced

1 cup chopped shallots
1 garlic clove, minced
5 parsley stalks
1 sprig fresh or pinch dried rosemary
1 sprig fresh or pinch dried thyme
1 medium bay leaf
1 cup vinegar
1 quart white wine
1½ quarts water
1 tablespoon salt
1 teaspoon peppercorns
2 tablespoons brown sugar

Heat oil in saucepan; add carrots and onion and cook to a golden brown. Add remaining ingredients and cook for 20 minutes. Let stand for 15 minutes; strain and cool before adding meats for marinating.

This marinade is less potent than uncooked marinades. *Yield:* 2½ quarts.

UNCOOKED MARINADE FOR MEATS AND VENISON

1 medium carrot, diced
1 medium onion, diced
1 tablespoon chopped shallots
4 parsley stalks
1 sprig fresh or pinch dried thyme
1 medium bay leaf
1 cup oil
1 cup vinegar

Combine all ingredients. *Yield:* approximately 1 quart.

VENISON

Vension is cooked like other red meats. See Roasting* and Braising* of beef, Pot Roast of Beef*.

ROAST CHICKEN FAMILY STYLE

1 three–four-pound drawn roasting chicken
Salt and pepper to taste
1 clove garlic, sliced
4 strips bacon
¼ pound butter or margarine
3 carrots, minced
4 outside celery stalks, minced
1 medium onion, minced
2 cups minced fresh mushrooms

Preheat oven to 375 degrees F. Wipe chicken with damp cloth; season with salt and pepper; insert garlic in meat; cover breast with bacon strips and butter or margarine and truss.

Place in heavy roasting pan and roast for 1 hour, basting all the while. Add vegetables and mushrooms and roast for another 45 minutes.

Place bird on large platter and carve. Serve vegetables as a side dish. *Yield:* 4 servings.

Notes: Chicken and vegetables should render sufficient juices for gravy, but if more is desired, add about half cup of water in the last 5 minutes of cooking.

To test if chicken is adequately cooked, lift the bird with heavy cooking fork in roasting pan, breast up, and if liquid coming out of chicken is perfectly clear, it is done.

If cooked in lightweight roasting pan, juices may evaporate more quickly; in that event add a little water to keep the vegetables moist during cooking time.

CREAMED CHICKEN

2 cups Basic Cream Sauce*
2 cups minced cooked chicken
Salt and pepper to taste
¼ cup dry sherry

Bring the Cream Sauce to a boil. Add the chicken; reduce heat and simmer for 10 minutes. Season with salt and pepper; add the dry sherry and serve. *Yield:* 4 servings.

POACHED CHICKEN WITH OYSTER SAUCE

1 three-pound chicken (drawn weight)
1 medium onion, chopped
1 carrot, diced
2 celery stalks, diced
1 sprig fresh or pinch dried thyme
1 small bay leaf
Salted water to cover
Oyster Sauce* (substitute Chicken Stock* for Fish
    Velouté*)

Place chicken and vegetables in pot just large enough to hold them. Add herbs and water. Bring to the boiling point and keep at low simmer for 1½ hours; do not overcook. Remove chicken to serving platter and keep warm. Serve with Oyster Sauce. *Yield:* approximately 4 servings.

CHICKEN PAPRIKA

1 three-pound frying chicken, cut into 8 pieces
1 teaspoon salt
⅛ teaspoon white pepper
3 tablespoons flour (any kind)
3 tablespoons butter or margarine
1 medium onion, chopped
1 tablespoon paprika
Pinch curry powder
1 quart Chicken Stock*
½ cup sour cream or non-dairy sour cream substitute
  at room temperature

Season chicken. Dredge in flour and fry in butter or margarine until golden brown. Add onions and cook with chicken for about 10–15 minutes. Add seasonings and Chicken Stock and cook an additional 45 minutes. Remove chicken to a warm platter. Bring gravy to a boil and add sour cream or non-dairy sour cream substitute. Mix well and pour over chicken. *Yield:* approximately 4 servings.

CHICKEN SAUTE NORMANDIE

1 three-pound frying chicken, cut into 8 pieces
Salt and pepper to taste
Flour for dredging (any kind)
4 tablespoons butter or margarine
Juice 1 lemon
½ cup dry white wine
1 pint 18 per cent cream (coffee cream) or non-dairy
  cream substitute
2 cups cooked buttered artichoke hearts

Preheat oven to 350 degrees F. Season chicken with salt and pepper. Dredge in flour. Sauté in butter or margarine until lightly colored. Bake about 1 hour. Remove chicken to serving dish and discard butter from pan in which chicken has been cooked. Add lemon juice and wine to pan and swill until pan juices are dissolved. Add cream or non-dairy cream substitute. Cook until liquid is reduced to half its original volume. Surround chicken with hot buttered artichoke hearts. Place sauce in gravy boat and serve. *Yield:* approximately 4 servings.

FEATHERED GAME

There are a great number of feathered game that can be eaten. For cooking purposes, they may be put into two classes:

1. Pheasants, red and gray partridge, hazel-hen, grouse and prairie fowl, wild ducks and teals, woodcocks and snipes.

2. Plovers, lapwings, sandpipers and water hens, the various quails.

PREPARATIONS FOR COOKING:

The birds of group 1 are better when aged for a few days at temperatures of about 50 degrees F., so that the flavor of their flesh can be heightened, increasing their culinary value. When fresh, the meat is flavorless.

Birds in group 2 do not need aging. Aging is, if anything, harmful to the flavor of the meat.

There are many ways to prepare and cook feathered game, but the most popular ways are roasting and braising. Old birds should be braised. Young birds should be roasted but not overdone or the breast meat will become dry.

ROAST FEATHERED GAME

Any young feathered game bird listed above
Salt and pepper to taste
4 tablespoons butter

Preheat oven to 400 degrees F. Young birds can be recognized by the grayish pink color of the legs and the tenderness of the keel bone (tip of the breast bone).

Draw and dry pluck the birds. Then pass them over a low flame to remove any pinfeathers or down. Wipe with a damp towel. Season with salt and pepper. Place the butter in the inner cavity and truss the legs of the bird. Place in roasting pan and roast until done. Allow 20 minutes per pound for pink (medium rare) and 25 minutes per pound for medium done. Serve with Orange Sauce*, Cumberland Sauce*, or Glazed Fruit*.

BRAISED FEATHERED GAME

Any older feathered game bird listed above
4 tablespoons butter or margarine
2 pounds sauerkraut, washed and well drained
½ pound salt pork
1 onion
1 carrot
1 cup dry white wine
10 peppercorns
½ teaspoon caraway seeds
Piece cheesecloth

Preheat oven to 350 degrees F. Prepare birds as for Roast Feathered Game*. Brown in butter or margarine on all sides in a frying pan. Place bird in a heavy casserole. Add the sauerkraut, salt pork, onion, carrot, and wine to the casserole. Tie the peppercorns and caraway seeds in the cheesecloth and add to the casserole. Bake for 1–1½ hours until bird is tender. Discard the onion and the cheesecloth bag. Quarter the bird. Place the sauerkraut on a serving platter and garnish it with the bird, salt pork, and carrots.

CHAPTER **13**

BREADS AND MUFFINS

Allergy Key: The two major sensitivities encountered in breads are wheat and yeast. In this chapter, several bread recipes are given using flours other than wheat. You will have to select those recipes using flours that are permitted in your particular allergy diet.

Note: Bread will shrink away from the side of the pan when done. Another test is to turn the bread out of the pan and tap the bottom. It will have a hollow sound if done.

PURE RYE BREAD

> 1 cake yeast
> 1 tablespoon blackstrap molasses
> 1¼ cups warm water (approximate)
> 4 cups rye flour
> 1 tablespoon salt
> 2 tablespoons oil
> ¼ cup caraway seeds (optional)

Dissolve the yeast and the molasses in 1 cup of the warm water. When yeast is dissolved, mix into the dry ingredients by hand. Add oil to mixture. Keep adding more water by the tablespoon until dough is the right consistency (so that all the flour mixes together, but is not too wet and gummy). If mixture becomes gummy, add small amounts of flour until dough is no longer sticky. Knead for 10 minutes, until the dough cleans the bowl. Cover the bowl with a folded towel and set in a pan of quite warm water, away from drafts or direct heat. Let rise for 1½ hours. Test by placing two fingers deep into dough. If the holes remain, the dough has risen enough. Punch down and knead for 3 or 4 minutes.

Preheat oven to 375 degrees F. Form dough into a loaf and place in greased 9-inch-square pan. If a hard crust is desired, brush top with water. Cover with towel and let rise again for about 20 minutes.

Bake for 1 hour and 15 minutes or until done. Cool a few minutes and then turn out on rack to cool. *Yield:* 1 loaf.

RYE AND BARLEY BREAD

   1 cake yeast
   1 tablespoon blackstrap molasses
   1¼ cups warm water (approximate)
   3 cups rye flour
   1 cup barley flour
   1 tablespoon salt
   ¼ cup caraway seeds (optional)
   2 tablespoons oil

Proceed as for Pure Rye Bread*, except this bread is baked in a rectangular, 8½-inch by 4½-inch bread baking pan, which should be greased.

Preheat oven to 375 degrees F. Bake for 65 minutes or until done. *Yield:* 1 loaf.

This bread is softer than the Pure Rye Bread.

RYE AND POTATO BREAD

1 cake yeast
1 tablespoon sugar
¾ cup warm water (approximate)
3 cups rye flour
1 cup mashed unseasoned potatoes (instant potatoes
* can be used)*
2 teaspoons salt
1 tablespoon oil
¼ cup caraway seeds (optional)

Proceed as for Pure Rye Bread*, substituting sugar for the molasses in the warm water. Mix mashed potatoes into the yeast and flour mixture before adding the oil. This bread is also baked in a greased 8½-inch by 4½-inch bread baking pan, like the Rye and Barley Bread*.

Preheat oven to 375 degrees F. Bake for 1 hour and 15 minutes or until done. Cool a few minutes and turn out on rack. *Yield:* 1 loaf.

This bread is higher and softer than the preceding two breads.

BARLEY AND POTATO BREAD

1 cake yeast
1 tablespoon sugar
¾ cup warm water (approximate)
3 cups barley flour
1 cup mashed unseasoned potatoes (instant potatoes
* can be used)*
2 tablespoons salt
1 tablespoon oil

Proceed as for Rye and Potato Bread*, substituting sugar for the molasses in the warm water. Bake in greased 8½-inch by 4½-inch bread baking pan.

Preheat oven to 375 degrees F. Bake for 1 hour and 15 minutes. Cool a few minutes in pan and turn out on a rack to cool. *Yield:* 1 loaf.

This bread will not hold together as well as the other breads in this chapter, but we have included it for those who are allergic to the other breads.

WHITE BREAD

> 1 *cake yeast*
> 2 *tablespoons sugar*
> 1½ *cups warm milk or non-dairy milk substitute*
> 4 *cups wheat flour*
> 1½ *tablespoons salt*

Proceed as for Pure Rye Bread*, substituting sugar for the molasses and the warm milk or non-dairy milk substitute for the water and omitting the oil.

Preheat the oven to 375 degrees F. Bake in greased 8½-inch by 4½-inch bread baking pan. Bake for 1 hour and 15 minutes or until done. Cool a few minutes and turn out on rack to cool. *Yield:* 1 loaf.

YEAST-FREE BREADS

Any of the foregoing bread recipes can be baked without yeast by adding ¾ cup of Rye Sourdough (recipe below), omitting the yeast, and reducing the water by about ½ cup.

RYE SOURDOUGH

2 cups rye flour
1 teaspoon salt
1 tablespoon sugar
2 cups cooled potato water (water that potatoes have
been cooked in)

Mix ingredients together and set in large china bowl. Cover lightly and let it sit and ferment in a warm place (perhaps near the stove or dishwasher) for 3 days before using to bake bread.

CORN BREAD

1½ cups cornmeal, white or yellow
⅓ cup cornstarch
2½ teaspoons baking powder
2 tablespoons sugar
¾ teaspoon salt
1 egg
3 tablespoons oil
¾ cup milk or non-dairy milk substitute

Preheat oven to 425 degrees F. Mix dry ingredients together. Beat egg and oil together and add to dry ingredients. Add milk or non-dairy milk substitute and mix thoroughly. Bake in greased 9-inch-square pan that has been heated in the oven for a few minutes before filling with corn bread for about 25 minutes.

BARLEY MUFFINS

¼ cup sugar
½ teaspoon salt
1½ cups barley flour

    5 teaspoons baking powder
    ¾ cup milk or non-dairy milk substitute
    4 tablespoons melted butter or margarine

Preheat oven to 375 degrees F. Sift dry ingredients. Add remaining ingredients. Mix well. Spoon into muffin tin that is either greased or lined with cupcake papers. Fill cups two-thirds full. Bake for about 30 minutes. *Yield:* 12 muffins.

CORN MUFFINS

Prepare Corn Bread* but bake in hot greased muffin tin, or one that has been lined with cupcake papers. Fill each cup two-thirds full.

CORNMEAL AND POTATO STARCH MUFFINS

    ⅔ cup cornmeal
    ⅓ cup potato starch
    2 teaspoons baking powder
    ½ teaspoon salt
    ½ teaspoon sugar
    1 egg
    ½ cup milk or non-dairy milk substitute
    1 teaspoon oil

Preheat oven to 400 degrees F. Sift dry ingredients together. Beat the egg slightly. Add milk or non-dairy milk substitute to the egg. Stir into the dry ingredients. Stir in the oil. Spoon into muffin tins that are either greased or lined with cupcake papers. Bake for 30 minutes. *Yield:* approximately 9 muffins.

ICE CREAM MUFFINS

1 cup potato starch
1 teaspoon baking powder
1 cup ice cream

Preheat oven to 425 degrees F. Combine ingredients and beat well. Place in muffin tins lined with cupcake papers. Bake for 20 minutes or until done. *Yield:* 12 muffins.

POTATO STARCH MUFFINS

4 eggs, separated
¼ teaspoon salt
1 tablespoon sugar
½ cup potato starch
1 teaspoon baking powder
2 tablespoons ice water

Preheat oven to 400 degrees F. Beat egg whites until stiff. Add salt and sugar to beaten yolks and fold this mixture into the whites. Sift dry ingredients together and beat into the eggs. Add ice water. Bake for 15 to 20 minutes. Bake either in greased muffin tins or use cupcake papers. *Yield:* 8–10 muffins.

MASHED POTATO AND RYE MUFFINS

1⅓ cups rye flour
4 teaspoons baking powder
¾ teaspoon salt
2 tablespoons sugar
⅔ cup unseasoned mashed potatoes (instant can be used)
1 cup water
2 tablespoons oil

Preheat oven to 400 degrees F. Sift dry ingredients into a bowl. Add mashed potatoes, water, and oil. Mix completely. Spoon into muffin tin that is either greased or lined with cupcake papers. Fill cups two-thirds full. Bake for 35–45 minutes until done. *Yield:* 12 muffins.

RICE FLOUR MUFFINS

> 1 cup rice flour
> 2 teaspoons baking powder
> ¼ teaspoon salt
> 1 teaspoon sugar
> 2 tablespoons oil
> ½ cup orange juice

Preheat oven to 400 degrees F. Combine dry ingredients. Stir in oil and orange juice. Form into small patties and place in greased muffin tin or tin lined with cupcake papers. Set aside for 10 minutes. Then bake for about 25 minutes. *Yield:* 9 muffins.

RICE AND RYE FLOUR MUFFINS

> ⅔ cup rice flour
> 1⅓ cups rye flour
> 4 teaspoons baking powder
> ¾ teaspoon salt
> 2 tablespoons sugar
> 1⅓ cups water
> 2 tablespoons oil

Preheat oven to 400 degrees F. Sift dry ingredients into a bowl. Add water and oil. Mix completely. Spoon into muffin tin that is either greased or lined with cupcake papers. Fill cups two-thirds full. Bake for 30–40 minutes until done. *Yield:* 12 muffins.

RICE FLOUR AND POTATO STARCH MUFFINS

1½ cups rice flour
⅓ cup potato starch
1 teaspoon salt
3 teaspoons baking powder
1 egg
1 cup milk or non-dairy milk substitute
3 tablespoons oil

Preheat oven to 400 degrees F. Sift dry ingredients together. Beat the egg slightly. Add milk or non-dairy milk substitute to the egg. Stir into the dry ingredients. Stir in the oil. Spoon into muffin tins that are either greased or lined with cupcake papers. Bake for 30 minutes. *Yield:* 12 muffins.

CHAPTER **14**

BAKED GOODS AND ICINGS

Allergy Key: Probably the greatest difference between allergy and non-allergy cooking will be apparent in this chapter. More than in any other chapter, different or unusual ingredients are needed here because most baked goods require flour and milk (two very common allergies). Such flours and starches as barley, potato and rice, and carob powder are used in many recipes in this chapter. Non-dairy milk-type substitutes as well as fruit juices and water are used for liquid. Many egg-free recipes have been included.

Because so many different ingredients are combined in baking, we thought it would be helpful to annotate each recipe with a list of what it does *not* include as well as giving a list of what it does include. Thus it will be easier for you to find recipes with the right combination of ingredients for your allergy problems. However, the absence of an ingredient is noted only when it would normally be present in the recipe. The presence of oil and non-dairy milk-type substitutes is also noted for the convenience of those who can cook only with oil, or those who cannot find a non-dairy milk-type substitute with acceptable ingredients. For a list of oils, see Chapter I.

Along with the unusual recipes you will also find many classic recipes in this chapter. Many of these, such as meringues, sponge cake, nut tortes, etc., are perfect for certain allergy diets without any changes.

You will find that baked goods are well worth the effort of making them, not only because they are delightful in themselves but also because it is much easier to stay on a restricted diet if there are also some special treats included in it. What child or adult will mind careful eating if his diet also includes Reese rolls, brownies, orange nut torte, meringue cookies, or any other of the enticing items presented in this chapter?

CAKES

Note: For cakes that require a greased pan, it is helpful to cut a piece of waxed paper to fit the pan and grease both the pan and the paper. In this way the cake comes out of the pan more easily.

NO-CHOCOLATE CHOCOLATE CAKE—I
NO MILK OR MILK SUBSTITUTE—NO WHEAT—NO CORN—NO CHOCOLATE—NO OIL—NO RYE

This is our favorite birthday cake—loved by young and old alike.

¾ cup butter or margarine
2½ cups sugar
1½ teaspoons vanilla
3 eggs
2 cups barley flour
1 cup carob powder
1½ teaspoons baking soda
¾ teaspoon salt
2 tablespoons strong black iced coffee
1½ cups minus 2 tablespoons ice water (if allergic
    to coffee, omit coffee and use 1½ cups ice water)

Preheat oven to 350 degrees F. Cream the butter or margarine; add sugar slowly; then add the vanilla and eggs. Beat until light and fluffy. Sift barley flour and carob powder, soda, and salt together; add these gradually, alternating with the iced coffee and ice water.

Pour into greased layer cake pans or loaf cake pan. Bake for 40–50 minutes. Test with toothpick. It toothpick comes out of center of cake dry, cake is done. Let cool in pans for 5 minutes. Loosen edges of cake and turn out onto cooling rack. *Yield:* 12–14 servings.

NO-CHOCOLATE CHOCOLATE CAKE—II

USES OIL—USES MILK OR MILK SUBSTITUTE—USES CORNSTARCH-FREE BAKING POWDER—NO WHEAT—NO CHOCOLATE—NO CORN—NO RYE

2 eggs at room temperature, separated
1½ cups sugar
1½ cups barley flour
¾ cup carob powder
2 teaspoons baking powder
1 teaspoon salt
⅓ cup cooking oil
1 cup milk or non-dairy milk substitute
1½ teaspoons vanilla

Preheat oven to 350 degrees F. Beat egg whites until frothy. Gradually add ½ cup sugar and beat until stiff. Set aside. Sift remaining sugar, barley flour, carob powder, baking powder, and salt together; add to this dry mixture, the oil, half of the milk or non-dairy milk substitute, and the vanilla. Beat until thoroughly mixed. Add remaining milk or non-dairy milk substitute and the 2 egg yolks and mix thoroughly again. Fold in the beaten egg whites.

Bake for 30–35 minutes in greased layer cake pans, 40–45 minutes for an oblong cake, and 30 minutes for cupcakes. Let cakes cool for a few minutes in the pans, then turn out on rack for complete cooling. *Yield:* 10–12 servings.

NO-CHOCOLATE CHOCOLATE CAKE—III
USES OIL—USES MILK OR MILK SUBSTITUTE—NO WHEAT—NO
CORN—NO CHOCOLATE—NO RYE

2 eggs at room temperature, separated
1½ cups sugar
1½ cups barley flour
¼ cup carob powder
¾ teaspoon baking soda
¾ teaspoon salt
⅓ cup oil
1 cup milk or non-dairy milk substitute

Preheat oven to 350 degrees F. Beat egg whites until frothy. Gradually add ½ cup sugar and beat until stiff. Set aside. Sift remaining sugar, barley flour, carob powder, soda, and salt together; add oil and ½ cup milk or non-dairy milk substitute and beat until thoroughly mixed. Add remaining ½ cup of milk or non-dairy milk substitute gradually and the 2 egg yolks and mix thoroughly again. Fold in egg whites.

Bake for 30–35 minutes in greased layer cake pans, 40–45 minutes for an oblong cake and 30 minutes for cupcakes. Let cakes cool for a few minutes in the pans, then turn out on rack for complete cooling. *Yield:* 10–12 servings.

EGG-FREE NO-CHOCOLATE CHOCOLATE CAKE
USES CREAM OR CREAM SUBSTITUTE—NO WHEAT—NO CORN—
NO EGG—NO CHOCOLATE—NO OIL—NO RYE

1 cup sugar
½ cup carob power
1 cup cream or non-dairy cream substitute
1 teaspoon soda dissolved in 3 tablespoons strong
   hot coffee or hot water

  1½ cups barley flour
  5 tablespoons melted butter or margarine
  1 teaspoon vanilla

Preheat oven to 350 degrees F. Mix sugar and carob powder. Add remaining ingredients and beat until thoroughly mixed. Pour batter into greased 9-inch-square pan and bake for 35 minutes or until a toothpick inserted in the center comes out clean. *Yield:* 8–10 servings.

ANGEL FOOD CAKE
NO MILK OR MILK SUBSTITUTE (OPTIONAL)—NO WHEAT—NO SHORTENING—NO OIL—NO RYE

  1 cup potato starch (or ⅔ cup cornstarch can be
    used)
  1½ cups sugar
  ½ teaspoon salt
  1¼ cups egg whites (about 10) at room temperature
  1 teaspoon cream of tartar
  ½ teaspoon vanilla
  ½ teaspoon almond extract

Preheat oven to 350 degrees F. Sift the potato starch, ½ cup of sugar, and the salt. Whip egg whites until foamy; add cream of tartar and whip until they stand in stiff peaks. Add remaining sugar 1 tablespoon at a time. Add vanilla and almond extracts. Slowly fold in the potato starch and sugar mixture. Pour into an ungreased 9-inch tube pan and bake about 45 minutes.

Cool by inverting pan on a rack as soon as cake comes out of the oven. This cake will probably fall out of the pan onto the rack because these starches are not as firm as wheat flour. The appearance of this cake will not be as high or light as a wheat flour cake either, but the flavor is every bit as good!

This cake is good served with Orange Sauce Icing*. *Yield:* 10–12 servings.

APPLESAUCE CAKE
NO MILK OR MILK SUBSTITUTE—NO WHEAT—NO CORN—NO EGGS
—NO OIL—NO RYE

> ½ cup butter or margarine
> 1 cup sugar
> 1½ cups Applesauce*
> 2¾ cups barley flour
> ½ teaspoon cinnamon
> ½ teaspoon cloves
> 1 teaspoon baking soda
> ¼ teaspoon salt

Preheat oven to 325 degrees F. Cream the butter or margarine and sugar together. Add the Applesauce. Sift the dry ingredients together and stir into the batter. Mix well and pour into a greased 8-inch-square baking pan. Bake for 50 minutes or until a toothpick inserted in the center comes out clean. Cool in the pan for 5 minutes, then turn out onto a rack. *Yield:* 8–10 servings.

LADY BALTIMORE CAKE
USES MILK OR MILK SUBSTITUTE—USES CORNSTARCH-FREE
BAKING POWDER—NO WHEAT—NO CORN—NO OIL—NO RYE

> ¾ cup butter or margarine
> 2 cups sugar
> 3 cups barley flour
> 3 teaspoons salt
> 3 teaspoons baking powder
> 1 cup milk or non-dairy milk substitute
> ¾ teaspoon vanilla
> ½ teaspoon lemon flavoring
> 6 egg whites at room temperature

Preheat oven to 350 degrees F. Cream butter or margarine and sugar together until light and fluffy. Sift dry ingredients into mixing bowl, alternating with the milk or non-dairy milk substitute. Add vanilla and lemon flavoring. Whip egg whites until they stand in stiff peaks; fold into the other mixture.

Bake in greased pans for about 30 minutes. If toothpick inserted in center of cake comes out clean, cake is done. Let cool in pans a few minutes and then turn out onto rack for cooling.

When cool, frost with White Icing*. *Yield:* 12–14 servings.

LORD BALTIMORE CAKE
USES MILK OR MILK SUBSTITUTE—NO WHEAT—NO CORN—NO OIL —NO RYE

1 cup butter or margarine
1¾ cups sugar
7 egg yolks at room temperature
3¼ cups barley flour
¼ teaspoon salt
1 teaspoon baking soda
2 teaspoons cream of tartar
½ teaspoon nutmeg
1 cup milk or non-dairy milk substitute
½ teaspoon lemon flavoring

Preheat oven to 350 degrees F. Cream butter or margarine and sugar together until mixed thoroughly. Add egg yolks, one at a time, beating thoroughly after each one. Sift the dry ingredients together and add them to the original mixture, alternating with the milk or non-dairy milk substitute. Add lemon flavoring.

Bake in greased pans for 35–40 minutes. Let cake cool in pans for a few minutes and then turn out on rack for complete cooling.

When cool, frost with Maple Icing*. *Yield:* 12–14 servings.

ORANGE ROLL

NO MILK OR MILK SUBSTITUTE (OPTIONAL)—NO WHEAT—NO CORN
—NO OIL—NO RYE

4 eggs at room   ⅓ cup ground almonds
   temperature   Grated rind ½ orange
4 tablespoons sugar

FILLING: *whipped cream or non-dairy whip topping, or thick jelly or jam.*

TO DECORATE: *Candied orange peel, shaved chocolate, or slivered almonds.*

Preheat oven to 400 degrees F. Separate the eggs. Beat the yolks by hand until light; gradually add the sugar, almonds, and grated orange rind. Beat the egg whites until stiff; fold them into egg yolk mixture.

Grease a jelly roll pan and line with greased waxed paper. Pour mixture into pan and bake for 12–15 minutes, until cake springs back from touch. While baking, warm a damp towel against the oven. When cake is removed from oven, cover with the towel and cool cake for about 10 minutes; then refrigerate for about 45 minutes.

Spread cake with whipped cream, non-dairy whip topping, or jelly or jam. Loosen the bottom from the paper with a knife. Roll with the aid of the waxed paper. Garnish top with the filling and decorate with candied orange peel, shaved chocolate, or slivered almonds. *Yield:* 8 servings.

NO-CHOCOLATE REESE ROLL
NO MILK OR MILK SUBSTITUTE (OPTIONAL)—NO WHEAT—NO
CORN—NO CHOCOLATE—NO OIL—NO RYE

4 eggs at room temperature
4 tablespoons sugar
½ teaspoon vanilla
2 tablespoons carob powder
1 tablespoon potato starch

FILLING: *whipping cream, non-dairy whip topping, or thick jelly or jam.*
TO DECORATE: *candy, shaved chocolate, or slivered almonds.*

Preheat oven to 350 degrees F. Separate the eggs. Beat the egg yolks with the sugar and vanilla. Beat the egg whites until stiff. Fold the whites into the yolks. Sift the carob powder and potato starch together and fold into the egg mixture.

Grease a loaf cake pan and line with greased waxed paper. Pour mixture into pan and bake for about 18 minutes. Cool. Spread with whipping cream, non-dairy whip topping, or jelly or jam. Loosen the bottom from the paper with a knife. Roll with the aid of the waxed paper. Garnish top with the filling and decorate with candy, shaved chocolate, or slivered almonds. *Yield:* 8 servings.

The following topping is also very good with it, but it contains chocolate, milk or milk substitute and corn.

1 square unsweetened chocolate
1 tablespoon butter or margarine
¼ cup warm water
¾ cup milk or milk substitute
½ cup sugar
1 tablespoon cornstarch

Melt chocolate and butter or margarine together over low heat. Add the warm water, the milk or milk substitute, sugar, and cornstarch, which have been already mixed together. Cook over low heat until thick. Cool and pour over Reese Roll*. *Yield:* 8 servings.

POTATO STARCH SPONGE CAKE
NO MILK OR MILK SUBSTITUTE—NO WHEAT—NO CORN—NO
SHORTENING—NO OIL—NO RYE

> *8 eggs at room temperature*
> *1½ cups sugar, sifted*
> *1½ tablespoons lemon juice*
> *1 lemon rind, grated*
> *¾ cup potato starch, sifted*
> *Dash salt*

Preheat oven to 350 degrees F. Separate 7 of the eggs. Beat the 7
yolks and the 1 whole egg until frothy. Gradually add the sugar,
lemon juice, and lemon rind, beating constantly and thoroughly.
Gradually add the potato starch, stirring constantly. In a separate
bowl, beat the egg whites with the salt until stiff but not dry. Fold
egg whites gently (by hand) into the egg yolk mixture, making
sure everything is mixed well.

Pour into 10-inch tube pan and bake for about 1 hour, until the
cake springs back when touched with a finger. Invert the cake pan
on cups or on a large ginger ale bottle until it is thoroughly cool;
then remove from pan.

Sponge cake can be topped with whipped cream or non-dairy
whip topping and fresh, frozen, or canned fruit. It is also good
served with Orange Sauce Icing*. *Yield:* 10–12 servings.

Note: Never scour a sponge cake pan with cleanser or detergent
of any kind. Simply wash thoroughly with hot water.

JELLY ROLL
NO MILK OR MILK SUBSTITUTE—NO WHEAT—NO CORN—NO
SHORTENING—NO OIL—NO RYE

> *4 eggs at room temperature*
> *¾ cup sugar, sifted*

2 teaspoons lemon juice
½ lemon rind, grated
¼ cup plus 1 tablespoon potato starch, sifted
Dash salt
½ cup jelly
Confectioners' sugar (optional)

Preheat oven to 350 degrees F. Separate 3 of the eggs. Beat the 3 yolks and the 1 whole egg until frothy. Gradually add the sugar, lemon juice, and lemon rind, beating constantly and thoroughly. Gradually add the sifted potato starch, stirring constantly. In a separate bowl, beat the egg whites with the salt until stiff but not dry. Fold egg whites gently (by hand) into the egg yolk mixture, making certain everything is mixed well.

Grease jelly roll pan; line with greased waxed paper. Bake for 35 minutes or until it springs back when touched with a finger. Immediately turn out upside down on rack to cool; remove paper. When cool, spread with jelly and roll. Top with sifted confectioners' sugar if desired. *Yield:* 6–8 servings.

RICE FLOUR SPONGE CAKE

Proceed as for Potato Starch Sponge Cake* but substitute rice flour for potato starch and reduce baking time by 10–15 minutes.

RICE FLOUR JELLY ROLL

Proceed as for Jelly Roll* but substitute rice flour for potato starch and reduce baking time 10–15 minutes.

COOKIES

BUTTER COOKIES
NO MILK OR MILK SUBSTITUTE—NO EGGS—NO OIL—NO RYE

1 cup butter or margarine
1 cup sifted confectioners' sugar
1 teaspoon vanilla
2¼ cups wheat flour
¼ teaspoon salt
Colored sugar, ground coconut, ground nuts, or
chocolate sprinkles (optional)

Mix first three ingredients thoroughly. Stir in flour and salt. Mix with hands. Shape into 2 rolls, about 2 inches in diameter. Roll one roll in colored sugar and the other in ground coconut or ground nuts or chocolate sprinkles. Chill several hours.

Preheat oven to 400 degrees F. Cut slices about ⅛ inch thick. Bake 8–10 minutes on an ungreased cookie sheet. *Yield:* approximately 4½ dozen cookies.

CINNAMON BUTTER COOKIES
NO MILK OR MILK SUBSTITUTE—NO EGGS—NO CORN—NO OIL— NO RYE

½ cup butter or margarine
1 cup brown sugar
¼ cup cold water
2 cups wheat flour
1 teaspoon baking soda
½ teaspoon salt
½ teaspoon cinnamon

Mix butter or margarine and sugar thoroughly. Stir in cold water. Blend in dry ingredients. Mix thoroughly with hands and shape into long roll. Chill until stiff (overnight is best).

Preheat oven to 400 degrees F. Cut in ¼-inch slices. Bake 6–8 minutes on an ungreased cookie sheet. *Yield:* approximately 4 dozen cookies.

BARLEY COOKIES
USES OIL—USES CORNSTARCH-FREE BAKING POWDER—NO MILK OR MILK SUBSTITUTE—NO WHEAT—NO CORN—NO RYE

2 eggs, beaten
½ cup oil
¾ cup sugar
1½ cups barley flour
¾ teaspoon baking powder
¼ teaspoon baking soda
½ teaspoon salt
¾ teaspoon vanilla

Preheat oven to 375 degrees F. Mix all the ingredients together thoroughly. Drop with a teaspoon onto a greased cookie sheet or a sheet lined with white shelf-lining paper. Bake for 10–15 minutes. *Yield:* approximately 3 dozen cookies.

CORNMEAL COOKIES
USES MILK OR MILK SUBSTITUTE (OPTIONAL)—NO WHEAT—NO OIL—NO RYE

⅓ cup butter or margarine
1 cup dark brown sugar, firmly packed
1 egg
3 tablespoons milk or non-dairy milk substitute or fruit juice
2 cups cornmeal
1 teaspoon vanilla

Preheat oven to 375 degrees F. This recipe can be made by hand mixing; an electric mixer is not necessary.

Cream butter or margarine and sugar. Add egg and beat well. Add remaining ingredients. Drop on a greased cookie sheet with a teaspoon and bake for 15 minutes. *Yield:* approximately 5 dozen cookies.

GINGERBREAD MEN
NO MILK OR MILK SUBSTITUTE—NO WHEAT—NO EGGS—NO OIL

¼ cup butter or margarine
½ cup sugar
½ cup blackstrap molasses
1¼ cups rye flour
1¼ cups cornstarch
1 teaspoon baking soda
¼ teaspoon ground cloves
¾ teaspoon cinnamon
¼ teaspoon ground ginger
½ teaspoon salt
½ cup hot water
Raisins (optional)

Preheat oven to 350 degrees F. Cream the butter or margarine and sugar; add molasses. Sift the dry ingredients together and add gradually, alternating with the water. As the mixture gets too thick for an electric mixer, finish the mixing by hand. If the dough gets too gummy, add more rye flour. Roll out on floured board or on greased cookie sheet. Cut out gingerbread men or any other pattern you wish to use. Decorate with raisins if desired. Bake for about 8 minutes, or until the cookie springs back when you press it. *Yield:* approximately 18 cookies.

When the cookies are cool, you can mix together: ¼ cup confectioners' sugar; few drops of water; food coloring.

Make a thick paste and use to decorate the cookies.

LEMON COOKIES
NO MILK OR MILK SUBSTITUTE—NO EGGS—NO OIL—NO RYE

1 cup butter or margarine
½ cup confectioners' sugar
1 teaspoon lemon or peppermint extract
2 cups wheat flour
¼ teaspoon salt

Preheat oven to 400 degrees F. Cream butter or margarine and the sugar. Add the lemon or peppermint extract and stir. Add dry ingredients. Mix well. Shape into half-inch balls and flatten slightly. Bake 8–10 minutes on an ungreased cookie sheet. *Yield:* approximately 3½ dozen cookies.

Meringue Note: Before beating egg whites, wash beaters in cold water to which 1 tablespoon each of salt and vinegar has been added. Dry and use.

MERINGUE COOKIES
NO MILK OR MILK SUBSTITUTE—NO WHEAT—NO CORN—NO SHORTENING—NO OIL—NO RYE

4 egg whites at room temperature
1 cup minus 1 tablespoon sugar
1 teaspoon vanilla

Preheat oven to 225 degrees F. Beat egg whites at high speed on electric mixer until frothy and white. Gradually add the sugar and vanilla. Beat until the mixture stands in stiff peaks. Make sure it is beaten enough, but stop immediately when stiff-peak stage is reached.

Line cookie sheet with white shelf-lining paper held down by Scotch tape; make drop cookies with a demitasse spoon. Bake for 60–70 minutes, depending on whether you want them chewy or crisp. *Yield:* approximately 8–9 dozen cookies.

BROWN SUGAR MERINGUE COOKIES
NO MILK OR MILK SUBSTITUTE—NO WHEAT—NO CORN—NO
SHORTENING—NO OIL—NO RYE

> *2 egg whites*
> *4 tablespoons brown sugar*
> *½ teaspoon vanilla*

Preheat oven to 225 degrees F. Beat egg whites at high speed on electric mixer until frothy and white. Gradually add the sugar and vanilla. Beat until the mixture stands in stiff peaks. Make sure it is beaten enough, but stop immediately when stiff-peak stage is reached.

Line cookie sheet with white shelf-lining paper held down by Scotch tape; make drop cookies with a demitasse spoon. Bake for 60–70 minutes, depending on whether you want them chewy or crisp. *Yield:* approximately 3 dozen cookies.

COCONUT MERINGUE COOKIES
NO MILK OR MILK SUBSTITUTE—NO WHEAT—NO CORN—NO
SHORTENING—NO OIL—NO RYE

> *2 eggs whites at room temperature*
> *4 tablespoons sugar*
> *½ teaspoon vanilla*
> *½ cup coconut*

Preheat oven to 225 degrees F. Prepare as for the previous two Meringue Cookie* recipes. When done, gently fold in the coconut by hand. Drop on cookie sheet lined with white shelf paper as in Meringue Cookie recipes. Bake for 60–70 minutes and let cool in the oven for an additional 5 minutes. *Yield:* approximately 4 dozen cookies.

NUT MERINGUE COOKIES
NO MILK OR MILK SUBSTITUTE—NO WHEAT—NO CORN—NO
SHORTENING—NO OIL—NO RYE

> 2 egg whites at room temperature
> 4 tablespoons sugar
> ½ teaspoon vanilla
> ½ cup ground almonds

Preheat oven to 225 degrees F. Prepare as for the previous Meringue Cookie* recipes. When done, gently fold in the nuts by hand. Drop on cookie sheet lined with white shelf paper as in Meringue Cookie recipes. Bake for 60–70 minutes and let cool in the oven for an additional 5 minutes. *Yield:* approximately 4 dozen cookies.

NUT BALLS
NO MILK OR MILK SUBSTITUTE—NO WHEAT—NO CORN—NO
SHORTENING—NO OIL—NO RYE

> 2 cups ground nuts
> 1 cup brown sugar
> 1½ cups flaked coconut
> 1 cup chopped dates or chopped candied cherries
> 2 eggs, beaten
> Coconut or nuts to roll cookies in

Preheat oven to 350 degrees F. Combine all the ingredients and mix thoroughly. Moisten hands and shape into balls about 1 inch in diameter. Roll in additional nuts or coconut. Place on well-greased cookie sheet and bake for 10–12 minutes. *Yield:* approximately 7–8 dozen cookies.

OATMEAL COOKIES
USES MILK OR MILK SUBSTITUTE (OPTIONAL)—NO WHEAT—NO
CORN—NO OIL—NO RYE

⅓ cup butter or margarine
1 cup dark brown sugar, firmly packed
1 egg
1½ tablespoons milk or non-dairy milk substitute or
   fruit juice
2 cups quick oats
1 teaspoon vanilla

Preheat oven to 375 degrees F. This recipe can be made by hand
mixing; an electric mixer is not necessary.

Cream butter or margarine and sugar. Add egg and beat well.
Add remaining ingredients. Drop on a greased cookie sheet with a
teaspoon and bake for 15 minutes. *Yield:* approximately 5 dozen
cookies.

PEANUT BUTTER COOKIES—I
USES CREAM OR CREAM SUBSTITUTE—NO WHEAT—NO EGGS—
NO SHORTENING—NO OIL—NO RYE

1 cup peanut butter
1 cup sugar
½ cup cream or non-dairy cream substitute or
   canned evaporated milk
4 teaspoons cornstarch

Preheat oven to 350 degrees F. Mix all ingredients together thoroughly. Drop by teaspoonful onto ungreased cookie sheet. Bake for
about 15 minutes. Cool a few minutes on the sheet; then remove to a
plate. *Yield:* approximately 4½ dozen cookies.

PEANUT BUTTER COOKIES—II
USES CORNSTARCH-FREE BAKING POWDER—NO MILK OR MILK
SUBSTITUTE—NO WHEAT—NO CORN—NO OIL—NO RYE

½ cup peanut butter
½ cup butter or margarine
½ cup white sugar
½ cup brown sugar
½ teaspoon baking powder
1 egg

Preheat oven to 350 degrees F. Cream peanut butter, butter or margarine, and sugars until mixture is light and fluffy; add baking powder and egg. Beat until smooth. Drop by the teaspoonful onto an ungreased cookie sheet about 2 inches apart. Bake for about 15 minutes, until edges are a dark brown. Cool for a few minutes on the sheet; then remove to a plate. *Yield:* approximately 4½ dozen cookies.

RICE OR BARLEY COOKIES
USES OIL—USES CORNSTARCH-FREE BAKING POWDER—NO EGGS—
NO MILK OR MILK SUBSTITUTE—NO WHEAT—NO CORN—NO RYE

¼ cup honey
⅓ cup oil
½ cup sugar
1 cup rice flour or barley flour
½ teaspoon baking powder
¼ teaspoon baking soda
¼ teaspoon salt
½ teaspoon vanilla

Preheat oven to 375 degrees F. Mix all the ingredients together thoroughly. Drop with a teaspoon onto a greased cookie sheet, or one covered with white shelf-lining paper. Bake for 12–15 minutes. *Yield:* approximately 3 dozen cookies.

SCOTCH SHORTBREAD
NO MILK OR MILK SUBSTITUTE—NO EGGS—NO CORN—NO OIL—NO RYE

¾ cup butter or margarine
¼ cup sugar
½ teaspoon vanilla
2 cups flour, sifted

Preheat oven to 350 degrees F. Cream the butter or margarine and the sugar; add vanilla. Work in the flour with your hand. If the dough is too crumbly, add small amounts of creamed butter or margarine until it can be rolled. Roll dough ⅓ inch thick. Cut into fancy shapes. Bake on ungreased cookie sheet for 20–25 minutes. Cookies will not be brown when done. *Yield:* approximately 2½ dozen medium-sized cookies.

BUTTERSCOTCH SHORTBREAD
NO MILK OR MILK SUBSTITUTE—NO EGGS—NO CORN—NO OIL—NO RYE

1 cup butter or margarine
½ cup brown sugar
¼ cup white sugar
1 teaspoon vanilla
2¼ cups wheat flour
1 teaspoon salt

Preheat oven to 300 degrees F. Cream the butter or margarine and the sugars; add vanilla. Work in the flour and salt with your hands. Roll dough ⅓ inch thick; cut into small cookies. Bake on ungreased cookie sheet for 25 minutes. *Yield:* approximately 4 dozen cookies.

VANILLA COOKIES
USES OIL—USES CORNSTARCH-FREE BAKING POWDER—NO MILK
OR MILK SUBSTITUTE—NO CORN—NO RYE

2 eggs, beaten
½ cup oil
¾ cup sugar
1½ cups wheat flour
¾ teaspoon baking
  powder

¼ teaspoon baking soda
½ teaspoon salt
¾ teaspoon vanilla

Preheat oven to 375 degrees F. Mix all the ingredients together thoroughly. Drop with a teaspoon onto a greased cookie sheet. Bake for 10–15 minutes. *Yield:* approximately 3 dozen cookies.

BROWNIES AND BARS

BUTTERSCOTCH BROWNIES
OIL MAY BE USED—USES CORNSTARCH-FREE BAKING POWDER—
NO MILK OR MILK SUBSTITUTE—NO WHEAT—NO CORN

1 cup brown sugar
¼ cup melted butter or margarine, cooled, or ¼ cup
  oil
1 egg
1 teaspoon vanilla
½ cup rye flour
1 teaspoon baking powder
½ teaspoon salt

Preheat oven to 350 degrees F. Mix sugar with butter or margarine or oil. Add egg and vanilla and beat well. Sift dry ingredients together and stir into the sugar-egg mixture. Pour into greased 9-inch-square pan and bake for 20–25 minutes.

NO-CHOCOLATE CHOCOLATE BROWNIES
OIL MAY BE USED—NO MILK OR MILK SUBSTITUTE—NO WHEAT—
NO CHOCOLATE—NO CORN—NO RYE

>   *3 eggs*
>   *½ teaspoon salt*
>   *2 cups sugar*
>   *½ cup melted and cooled butter or margarine, or*
>   *½ cup oil*
>   *⅔ cup barley flour*
>   *⅓ cup carob powder*

Preheat oven to 350 degrees F. This recipe can be mixed by hand without using an electric mixer. Beat the eggs and salt until light and foamy. Add the sugar gradually. Add the butter or margarine or oil and mix slightly. Sift the barley flour and carob powder together and fold them into the mixture by hand. Pour into greased 9-inch-square pan. Bake for about 35 minutes. These brownies will not harden. They will be soft and chewy.

OATMEAL BARS
NO MILK OR MILK SUBSTITUTE—NO WHEAT—NO EGGS—NO OIL—
NO RYE

>   *½ cup melted and cooled butter or margarine*
>   *2 cups quick oats*
>   *½ cup firmly packed light brown sugar*
>   *¼ cup white corn syrup*
>   *½ teaspoon salt*
>   *1½ teaspoons vanilla*

Preheat oven to 450 degrees F. Blend all the ingredients well and pack into greased 9-inch-square pan. Bake for 12 minutes. The pan should be lined with aluminum foil because this recipe will be sticky.

PIES

PIE SHELL
NO MILK OR MILK SUBSTITUTE—NO WHEAT—NO CORN—NO
EGGS—NO OIL—NO RYE

> 1½ cups fine crumbs made from any breakfast cereal
>   to which you are not allergic
> ½ cup melted butter or margarine
> ¼ cup sugar—to be used only if unsweetened cereal
>   is used

Mix all ingredients together. Line pie pan with mixture by pressing it firmly into place. Chill in refrigerator for 20 minutes. Then fill with any desired filling.

BARLEY FLOUR PIE CRUST
USES CORNSTARCH-FREE BAKING POWDER—NO MILK OR MILK
SUBSTITUTE—NO WHEAT—NO CORN—NO EGGS—NO OIL—NO RYE

> 1½ cups barley flour
> 1 teaspoon baking powder
> ½ teaspoon salt
> 4 tablespoons butter, margarine, or shortening
> 6 tablespoons fruit juice

Preheat oven to 400 degrees F. Sift dry ingredients together. Cut in butter, margarine, or shortening. Add fruit juice and mix to a stiff dough. Line board with waxed paper and dust paper with barley flour. Roll out dough, then transfer to 9-inch pie shell by lifting paper and fitting dough into shell. Remove paper, trim crust, and prick bottom with a fork in several places. Bake for 12–14 minutes.

COCONUT CRUST
NO MILK OR MILK SUBSTITUTE—NO WHEAT—NO CORN—NO EGGS
—NO OIL—NO RYE

3 tablespoons butter or margarine, melted
3½ ounces coconut

Preheat oven to 300 degrees F. Mix ingredients and spread evenly on bottom and sides of 9-inch pie pan. Bake for 20 minutes.

CHOCOLATE COCONUT CRUST
USES CHOCOLATE—NO MILK OR MILK SUBSTITUTE—NO WHEAT—
NO EGGS—NO OIL—NO RYE

2 tablespoons butter or margarine
2 one-ounce squares unsweetened chocolate
2 tablespoons hot coffee
⅔ cup confectioners' sugar
1½ cups shredded coconut

Combine butter or margarine and chocolate in a double boiler. Cook and stir until all the chocolate is melted. Add hot coffee and sugar. Stir in well. Fold in coconut. Pour into greased 9-inch pie pan and spread evenly on bottom and sides. Refrigerate until firm.

RICE FLOUR PIE CRUST
NO MILK OR MILK SUBSTITUTE—NO WHEAT—NO CORN—NO EGGS
—NO OIL—NO RYE

¾ cup rice flour
½ teaspoon salt
4 tablespoons butter or margarine
½ cup orange juice at room temperature

Preheat oven to 350 degrees F. Mix dry ingredients. Work butter or margarine into them. Add orange juice and knead into a solid mass. Turn out on waxed-paper-lined board, dusted with rice flour. Let dough rest for 10 minutes; then roll out. Lift waxed paper with dough onto 9-inch pie pan. Fit dough onto pan and remove waxed paper. Prick bottom of crust in several places with a fork. Bake for about 20 minutes until done.

MINCEMEAT PIE
NO MILK OR MILK SUBSTITUTE—NO WHEAT—NO CORN—NO EGGS —NO OIL—NO RYE

½ pound beef suet, chopped
10 ounces cooked, finely diced beef tenderloin
1 cup each raisins, currants, and white raisins
1 cup chopped Candied Orange or Grapefruit
  Peel*
Juice 1 orange
Peel 1 orange, chopped
½ cup peeled, chopped apples
1 tablespoon ground allspice
⅛ cup each brandy, Jamaica rum, and Madeira wine
  (⅜ cup cider or orange juice can be substituted
  for brandy, rum, and wine)
1 unbaked 9-inch Pie Shell* and top crust (see
  p. 179ff)

Mix thoroughly all ingredients, except the pie shell and crust. Place in earthenware jar and store in cool place for 30 days before using.

Preheat oven to 400 degrees F. Line 9-inch pie tin with pastry dough. Pour in mixture and cover top with crust. Bake for 35 minutes or until crust is well browned.

FRESH FRUIT PIE
NO MILK OR MILK SUBSTITUTE—NO WHEAT—NO CORN—NO EGGS
—NO OIL—NO RYE

    2 cups cut up fresh fruit
    ½ cup fruit juice (any kind)
    2½ tablespoons tapioca
    ⅛ teaspoon salt
    ¾–1 cup sugar
    ½ teaspoon vanilla
    1 unbaked 9-inch Pie Shell*

Preheat oven to 425 degrees F. Combine first six ingredients in a bowl. Let stand for 15 minutes. Pour into pie shell. Bake for 35–45 minutes.

CRANBERRY PIE
NO MILK OR MILK SUBSTITUTE—NO WHEAT—NO OIL—NO RYE

    2 cups sugar
    1 cup water
    1 pound fresh cranberries
    2 tablespoons cornstarch
    ¼ teaspoon salt
    3 tablespoons butter or margarine, melted
    2 egg yolks, beaten
    1 baked 9-inch Pie Shell*

Preheat oven to 325 degrees F. Cook sugar and ¾ cup water until sugar is dissolved. Add cranberries and cook until they stop popping. Combine cornstarch, remaining water, salt, butter or margarine, and egg yolks, and add 3 tablespoons of the cooked cranberries. Mix thoroughly. Add to remaining cranberries and cook until thickened. When the mixture is thick and clear, cook an additional 5 minutes. Pour into pastry shell and bake for 15–18 minutes.

PUMPKIN PIE—I
USES MILK OR MILK SUBSTITUTE—NO WHEAT—NO CORN—NO
SHORTENING—NO OIL—NO RYE

2 eggs, slightly beaten
2 cups canned pumpkin
¾ cup dark brown sugar
½ teaspoon salt
1 tablespoon pumpkin pie spice
1⅔ cups milk or non-dairy milk substitute
½ teaspoon vanilla
1 unbaked 9-inch Pie Shell*

Preheat oven to 425 degrees F. Mix ingredients in order given. Pour into pastry shell. Bake for 15 minutes; reduce temperature to 350 degrees F. and continue baking 45–55 minutes or until knife inserted in center comes out clean.

PUMPKIN PIE—II
USES MILK OR MILK SUBSTITUTE—NO WHEAT—NO EGGS—NO
SHORTENING—NO OIL—NO RYE

¾ cup brown sugar
1 cup canned pumpkin
2 tablespoons cornstarch
1 tablespoon pumpkin pie spice
2 cups milk or non-dairy milk substitute
1 baked 9-inch Pie Shell*

Preheat oven to 325 degrees F. Mix first five ingredients together. Cook until thickened, stirring constantly (about 20 minutes). Pour into baked pie shell. Bake for 15 minutes. Cool. Refrigerate.

SWEET POTATO PIE
USES MILK OR MILK SUBSTITUTE—NO WHEAT—NO CORN—NO
SHORTENING—NO OIL—NO RYE

> 1 cup cooked mashed sweet potatoes
> 2 small bananas, peeled and mashed
> 1 cup milk or non-dairy milk substitute
> 2 tablespoons sugar
> ½ teaspoon salt
> 2 egg yolks, beaten
> 3 tablespoons finely chopped raisins
> ½ teaspoon nutmeg
> 1 baked 9-inch Pie Shell* (optional)

Preheat oven to 300 degrees F. Combine sweet potatoes and
bananas; add milk or non-dairy milk substitute and blend thoroughly. Add sugar, salt, egg yolks, raisins, and nutmeg. Mix well.
Pour into well-greased 9-inch pie pan or onto a baked pie shell.
Bake for about 45 minutes or until pie is set and firm to the touch;
the top should be golden brown.

PASTRY
USES MILK OR MILK SUBSTITUTE—NO WHEAT—NO CORN—NO OIL

> ½ cup butter or margarine
> 1 cup milk or non-dairy milk substitute
> 1 package yeast
> 2 cups barley flour
> 1 cup rye flour
> 1 teaspoon salt
> ½ cup sugar
> 3 egg yolks, well beaten
> Filling (see suggested fillings below)
> Confectioners' sugar (optional)

Melt butter or margarine together with milk or non-dairy milk substitute; cool to lukewarm. Add crumbled yeast. Sift the flours and salt into a bowl. Add the sugar, milk mixture, and the well-beaten egg yolks. Beat until the dough leaves the sides of the bowl. Cover tightly and refrigerate at least overnight.

Preheat oven to 375 degrees F. Turn out on floured waxed paper on a board and let rest for 10 minutes. Divide into 3 parts and roll as thin as possible. Fill with desired filling and roll up and place on cookie sheet lined with white shelf-lining paper. Let rise for 1 hour. Bake for 25–35 minutes. When cool, sprinkle with confectioners' sugar if desired. Slice in half-inch slices. *Yield:* approximately 4–5 dozen pieces.

SUGGESTED FILLINGS:

any kind of preserve or jam
lekvar (prune jam)
poppy seed mixture
cinnamon and sugar
raisins and sugar
nuts and sugar

CORNSTARCH PUFF PASTE
USES MILK OR MILK SUBSTITUTE—NO WHEAT—NO OIL—NO RYE

1½ cups milk or non-dairy milk substitute
2 tablespoons butter or margarine
⅔ cup cornstarch
Dash salt
5 eggs
Filling: whipped cream, non-dairy whip topping,
*   custard, ice cream, or preserves*

Preheat oven to 425 degrees F. Place 1 cup of milk or non-dairy milk substitute and butter or margarine in a saucepan and bring to a boil. Meanwhile, dilute the cornstarch in the remaining half cup of milk and stir until smooth. Add dash of salt. Remove milk from fire and stir cornstarch solution into it, using a wooden spoon. Return mixture to a low fire and stir constantly until mixture is very thick. Remove from fire. Add 1 egg at a time, beating until it is completely absorbed before adding another egg. Drop with a teaspoon onto a greased cookie sheet dusted with cornstarch, or make circle rings with pastry tube.

Bake for 10 minutes; then reduce heat to 350 degrees F. and bake an additional 20 minutes.

Cool and split the puffs sideways. Fill with whipped cream, non-dairy whip topping, custard, ice cream, or preserves. If circles are made, use as a cake layer and fill between them. *Yield:* approximately 2½ dozen puffs or 8 circles.

CHARLOTTE RUSSE
USES CHOCOLATE—WHIPPED CREAM OR NON-DAIRY WHIP
TOPPING (OPTIONAL)—NO OIL—NO RYE

12–15 ladyfingers
2 4-ounce bars German's sweet chocolate
4 tablespoons confectioners' sugar
4 tablespoons water and 1 teaspoon vanilla
  or
2 tablespoons water and 2 tablespoons strong black
  coffee
4 eggs, separated
Whipped cream or non-dairy whip topping (optional)
Shaved chocolate

Line a mixing bowl with waxed paper. Split ladyfingers and line sides and bottom of bowl with them. Melt together the chocolate, sugar, and liquid. Let cool. Add beaten egg yolks to chocolate mixture and blend well. Beat egg whites until stiff; stir into chocolate mixture until smooth. Pour into bowl lined with ladyfingers and refrigerate overnight.

To serve, turn out onto plate. Cover with whipped cream or non-dairy whip topping if desired; top with shaved chocolate. *Yield:* approximately 8 servings.

CHOCOLATE MOUSSE
USES CHOCOLATE—WHIPPED CREAM OR NON-DAIRY WHIP
TOPPING (OPTIONAL)—NO WHEAT—NO OIL—NO RYE

Make Charlotte Russe* mixture and pour into bowl lined only with waxed paper and put into freezer. Take out of freezer and un-mold 15 minutes before serving. Top with whipped cream or non-dairy whip topping and shaved chocolate if desired. *Yield:* approximately 8 servings.

ICINGS

BUTTERSCOTCH ICING
USES MILK OR MILK SUBSTITUTE—NO EGGS—NO CORN—NO
WHEAT—NO OIL—NO RYE

1½ cups firmly packed light brown sugar
1½ cups white sugar
1½ cups milk or non-dairy milk substitute
2 tablespoons butter or margarine

Cook sugars and milk or non-dairy milk substitute over low heat, stirring until sugars are dissolved. Then cook without stirring until a small amount will form a very soft ball when tried in cold water, 232 degrees F. on candy thermometer. Remove from heat and add butter or margarine. Let cool to lukewarm. Beat until creamy and thick enough to spread. If necessary, place frosting over hot water to keep soft while spreading.

MAPLE ICING
USES CREAM OR CREAM SUBSTITUTE—NO CORN—NO EGGS—NO
SHORTENING—NO WHEAT—NO OIL—NO RYE

2 cups sugar
1 cup cream or non-dairy cream substitute
½ teaspoon maple extract

Boil sugar and cream or non-dairy cream substitute together over
high heat 3 minutes without stirring. Reduce heat, continue cooking
until syrup reaches soft-ball stage, 232 degrees F. on candy thermometer, about a half hour. Wipe any crystals from sides of pan
gently but do not stir or frosting will be sugary. Let cool. Add maple
extract. Beat until creamy and of spreading consistency. If frosting
becomes too thick, add a small amount of milk or non-dairy milk
substitute and beat smooth.

WHITE ICING
NO MILK OR MILK SUBSTITUTE—NO WHEAT—NO SHORTENING—
NO OIL—NO RYE

2 egg whites
1½ cups sugar
5 tablespoons water
2 teaspoons light corn syrup
1 teaspoon vanilla

Mix unbeaten egg whites, sugar, water, and corn syrup in top of
double boiler. Beat with rotary beater until sugar is dissolved. Place
over boiling water and cook, beating constantly until frosting stands
in peaks, 6–7 minutes by hand, about 4 minutes with electric beaters.
Remove from heat. Add vanilla and beat until thick enough to
spread.

ORANGE SAUCE ICING
USES CREAM OR CREAM SUBSTITUTE—NO EGGS—NO CORN—NO
SHORTENING—NO WHEAT—NO OIL—NO RYE

1 can frozen orange juice, undiluted
½ pint whipping cream or non-dairy whipping cream
substitute

Thaw orange juice. Whip the cream or non-dairy whipping cream substitute and fold in the orange juice. Serve as a sauce. Good on Angel Food Cake* and Potato Starch and Rice Flour Sponge Cakes*.

CHAPTER 15

ICES, ICE CREAM, AND PUDDINGS

Allergy Key: This chapter contains some delightful recipes that help solve many allergy problems. Very few of the recipes require wheat; the ices contain no milk and can be made without eggs; the ice creams can be made with non-dairy milk substitutes; and cane sugar is used, whereas in commercial preparations corn sugar is used for sweetening.

ICES

CHERRY WATER ICE
NO MILK—NO CORN—NO EGGS

> 1 quart water
> 2¾ cups sugar
> 1½ cups cherry juice

Bring water and sugar to a boil. Cool. Add cherry juice and freeze. If sweetened cherry juice is used, reduce sugar to 2 cups. *Yield:* approximately 2 quarts.

CURRANT ICE
NO MILK—NO CORN—NO EGGS

> 3 pints red currants
> 1 pint red raspberries
> 1 cup water
> 1½ cups sugar

Place the currants, raspberries, and water in a saucepan and simmer for a few minutes. Strain. Add the sugar. Cool and freeze. *Yield:* approximately 1 quart.

APRICOT WATER ICE
NO MILK—NO CORN—NO EGGS

> 2¼ cups sugar
> 1 quart water
> 1½ to 1¾ cups fresh, canned, or frozen apricots

Bring the sugar and water to a fast boil. If canned apricots are used, reduce the sugar to 1½ cups. Crush apricots to a pulp and strain; add to water. Cool and freeze. *Yield:* approximately 2 quarts.

APRICOT MERINGUE ICE
NO MILK—NO CORN

> 2¼ cups sugar
> 1 quart water
> 1½ to 1¾ cups fresh, canned, or frozen apricots
> 1 egg white

Prepare the first three ingredients as in Apricot Water Ice*. If canned apricots are used, reduce the sugar to 1½ cups. When the mixture is frozen to a slush, mix in the egg white, which has been beaten until stiff. Mix occasionally while complete freezing is taking place, to prevent separation. *Yield:* approximately 2 quarts.

GRAPE WATER ICE
NO MILK—NO CORN—NO EGGS

Proceed as in Cherry Water Ice*, but substitute grape juice for cherry juice. *Yield:* approximately 2 quarts.

LIME WATER ICE
NO MILK—NO CORN—NO EGGS

> 2 cups sugar
> 1 quart water
> ¾ cup fresh lime juice, about 5 limes
> 2 drops green food coloring (check label for
>   possible allergy)
> Pinch salt

  Combine sugar and water in saucepan; bring to a boil and cook on fast fire for 5 minutes. Stir in lime juice and green coloring, and salt. Cool. Freeze. *Yield:* approximately 1½ quarts.

LIME MERINGUE ICE
NO MILK—NO CORN

> 2 cups sugar
> 1 quart water
> ¾ cup fresh lime juice, about 5 limes
> 2 drops green food coloring (check label for
>   possible allergy)
> Pinch salt
> 4 egg whites

  Prepare the first five ingredients as in Lime Water Ice*. When the mixture is frozen to a slush, mix in the egg whites, which have been beaten until stiff. Mix occasionally while complete freezing is taking place to prevent separation. *Yield:* approximately 2 quarts.

LEMON WATER ICE
NO MILK—NO CORN—NO EGGS

  Prepare as for Lime Water Ice*, but substitute lemon juice for lime juice and yellow food coloring for green food coloring. Check food coloring label for possible allergy.

LEMON MERINGUE ICE
NO MILK—NO CORN

Prepare as for Lime Meringue Ice*, but substitute lemon juice for lime juice and yellow food coloring for green food coloring. Check food coloring label for possible allergy.

NECTARINE WATER ICE
NO MILK—NO CORN—NO EGGS

Proceed as in Apricot Water Ice*, but substitute nectarines for apricots.

NECTARINE MERINGUE ICE
NO MILK—NO CORN

Proceed as in Apricot Meringue Ice*, but substitute nectarines for apricots.

PEACH WATER ICE
NO MILK—NO CORN—NO EGGS

Proceed as in Apricot Water Ice*, but substitute peaches for apricots.

PEACH MERINGUE ICE
NO MILK—NO CORN

Proceed as in Apricot Meringue Ice*, but substitute peaches for apricots.

RASPBERRY WATER ICE
NO MILK—NO CORN—NO EGGS

1 quart fresh raspberry juice
2¼ cups sugar
Juice 1 lemon

Combine all the ingredients and freeze. *Yield:* approximately 1 quart.

WATERMELON ICE
NO MILK—NO CORN—NO EGGS

2 cups water
1¼ cups sugar
4 cups peeled, diced, and deseeded watermelon
1 six-ounce can concentrated pink lemonade
1 cup peeled, diced, and deseeded watermelon for
*   garnish (optional)*
Mint for garnish (optional)

Combine water and sugar in a saucepan. Bring to a boil and boil for 5 minutes. Cool. Press watermelon through a sieve or purée in a blender. Add sugar syrup and pink lemonade to puréed watermelon. Freeze. *Yield:* approximately 1½ quarts.

CANTALOUPE ICE
NO MILK—NO CORN—NO EGGS

Prepare as for Watermelon Ice*, but substitute cantaloupe for watermelon, and concentrated orange juice for pink lemonade.

HONEYDEW ICE
NO MILK—NO CORN—NO EGGS

Prepare as for Watermelon Ice*, but substitute honeydew for watermelon, and concentrated limeade for pink lemonade.

LEMON SHERBET
USES CREAM OR NON-DAIRY CREAM SUBSTITUTE—NO CORN—NO EGGS

> 1 quart water
> 2¼ cups sugar
> 1¼ cups lemon juice
> 1 teaspoon lemon extract
> ½ cup 36 per cent cream (whipping cream) or
> non-dairy whipping cream substitute

Combine water and sugar and bring to a boil. Cool. Add remaining ingredients. Strain and freeze. *Yield:* approximately 2 quarts.

ORANGE SHERBET
USES CREAM OR NON-DAIRY CREAM SUBSTITUTE—NO CORN—NO EGGS

Prepare as for Lemon Sherbet*, but substitute orange juice for lemon juice and use orange extract instead of lemon extract.

BURNT ALMOND MAPLE MOUSSE
USES WHIPPING CREAM OR NON-DAIRY WHIPPING CREAM
SUBSTITUTE—NO CORN

 ½ cup sugar
 2 tablespoons water
 ¼ pound blanched almonds
 5 egg yolks
 ¾ cup maple syrup
 2 cups unsweetened whipping cream or non-dairy
    whipping cream substitute

Prepare burnt almonds ahead of time as follows: Place sugar and water in saucepan and cook until mixture is golden brown. Add almonds and stir. Pour onto greased cookie sheet to cool. Grind finely through meat grinder.

Place the egg yolks and maple syrup in top of a double boiler and cook over boiling water until thick and creamy. Remove from fire and stir until cold. Stir in whipping cream or non-dairy whipping cream substitute. Spoon into sherbet glasses and refrigerate until serving. *Yield:* approximately 4 servings.

ICE CREAMS

LEMON ICE CREAM
USES CREAM OR NON-DAIRY CREAM SUBSTITUTE—NO CORN

 1 quart 18 per cent cream (coffee cream) or
    non-dairy cream substitute
 1⅛ cups sugar
 3 eggs
 1 tablespoon lemon extract

Combine the first three ingredients and bring to a boil. Strain. Add lemon extract and freeze. *Yield:* approximately 1½ quarts.

PEACH ICE CREAM
USES CREAM OR NON-DAIRY CREAM SUBSTITUTE—NO CORN

12 ripe peaches, peeled and crushed
2 cups sugar
1 quart 18 per cent cream (coffee cream) or
  non-dairy cream substitute
2 eggs
1 teaspoon almond extract

Combine first four ingredients in a saucepan. Bring to a boil. Remove from fire and strain. Save peach pulp. Freeze until nearly frozen; then remove and add almond extract and peach pulp. Freeze completely. *Yield:* approximately 2 quarts.

PUDDINGS

BAKED MERINGUE PUDDING
NO MILK

¾ cup sugar
4 tablespoons water
8 egg whites
Pinch cream of tartar
1 pound confectioners' sugar

Preheat oven to 350 degrees F. Cook sugar and water in heavy saucepan, until golden brown. Pour into 2-quart pudding mold and tilt mold all around so as to coat it with the caramelized sugar. Set to cool. Rinse beaters in 1 quart cold water containing 1 tablespoon of salt and vinegar. Dry them. Beat egg whites with cream of tartar until stiff. Fold in confectioners' sugar and blend completely. Pour into pudding mold and place in a pan of hot water to bake. Bake for 25 minutes. Remove from oven. Cool and unmold. Serve with sliced fresh fruit if desired. *Yield:* approximately 6 servings.

PLUM PUDDING
NO MILK

>½ *pound beef suet, chopped*
>2 *cups bread crumbs (from any kind of bread)*
>1¾ *cups flour (any kind)*
>½ *cup peeled, chopped apple*
>½ *cup each malaga raisins, currants, and white raisins*
>1 *tablespoon chopped orange rind*
>1 *tablespoon chopped lemon rind*
>1 *tablespoon ginger*
>¼ *cup chopped almonds*
>1 *cup confectioners' sugar*
>*Juice 1 orange*
>*Rind 1 orange, chopped*
>4 *eggs*
>⅜ *cup Jamaica rum or brandy*
>1 *teaspoon salt*
>½ *teaspoon nutmeg*
>½ *teaspoon cinnamon*
>¼ *teaspoon cloves*
>*Warm brandy, if desired*

Mix all the ingredients except warm brandy thoroughly. Pour into greased mold. Wrap mold in greased cheesecloth; tie securely with string and place in covered double boiler or steam in 300 degree F. oven for 3 hours. When ready to serve, sprinkle pudding with brandy and ignite. *Yield:* approximately 10 servings.

CHAPTER 16

CANDIES

Allergy Key: A few candy recipes have been included in this book for those with allergies to the corn sugar, cottonseed and soybean oils, wheat, and preservatives present in many commercial candies.

COCONUT CREAM CANDY

1 tablespoon butter or margarine
1½ cups sugar
½ cup milk or non-dairy milk substitute
⅓ cup coconut
½ teaspoon vanilla

Melt butter or margarine in saucepan. Add sugar and milk or non-dairy milk substitute. Stir until sugar is completely dissolved. Bring to a boil and boil to 270 degrees F. on a candy thermometer. Remove from fire. Add coconut and vanilla and beat with a wooden spoon until thick and creamy. Pour into a greased 8-inch by 8-inch pan. Cut into squares when cooled. *Yield:* approximately 25.

NO-CHOCOLATE CHOCOLATE FUDGE

2 cups sugar
¾ cup milk or non-dairy milk substitute
¼ cup carob powder
¼ cup coffee
3 tablespoons butter or margarine
1 teaspoon vanilla
½ cup chopped nuts (optional)

Combine the first five ingredients in a saucepan. Bring to a boil.
Stir until mixture is smooth. Boil to 240 degrees F. on a candy
thermometer, soft-ball stage. Remove from fire and beat with a
wooden spoon until thick and creamy. Stir in vanilla and nuts. Pour
into greased 8-inch by 8-inch pan. Cool until hard. Cut into squares.
Yield: approximately 25.

CANDIED ORANGE PEEL

4 thin-skinned oranges
Cold water
1 cup sugar
½ cup water
Sugar to roll rinds in

Quarter the oranges and remove the rind. Grate rind slightly.
Place rind in saucepan and cover with cold water. Bring to boil and
continue a soft boil for 10 minutes. Discard the water and add cold
water to cover. Boil again for 10 minutes and remove peels. Allow to
cool until the white can be scraped off. Cut into thin strips. Boil the
sugar and water to 230 degrees F. on a candy thermometer, thread
stage, and add the peels. Cook the peels until all the liquid is absorbed and the peels are transparent, about 30 minutes. Stir occasionally to keep from burning. Roll in sugar and place on rack to
cool. Yield: approximately 15 dozen.

CANDIED GRAPEFRUIT PEEL

Proceed as for Candied Orange Peel* but substitute 2 grapefruits for the 4 oranges. *Yield:* approximately 13 dozen.

PEANUT BUTTER FUDGE

2 cups sugar
⅔ cup milk or non-dairy milk substitute
4 tablespoons peanut butter
1 teaspoon vanilla
Dash salt

Combine sugar and milk or non-dairy milk substitute in a saucepan. Bring to a boil and continue boiling to 240 degrees F. on a candy thermometer, soft-ball stage. Remove from heat. Add peanut butter, vanilla, and salt and beat with a wooden spoon until thick and creamy. Pour into a greased 8-inch by 8-inch pan. Cool and cut into squares. *Yield:* approximately 25.

MINTS

½ cup water
1½ cups sugar
4 drops oil of peppermint (available at drugstores)
2 drops food coloring (check label for possible allergy)

Boil water and sugar to 260 degrees F. on a candy thermometer. Remove from heat and add oil of peppermint and food coloring. Beat with wooden spoon until mixture begins to thicken. Drop with demitasse spoon onto greased waxed paper. Cool completely. *Yield:* approximately 4 dozen.

PENUCHE

1 tablespoon butter or margarine
2 cups brown sugar
⅓ cup cream or non-dairy cream substitute
¾ cup chopped salted nuts (almonds, peanuts,
    pecans, walnuts)
1 teaspoon vanilla

Melt butter or margarine in a saucepan. Add sugar and cream or non-dairy cream substitute. Bring to a boil and continue boiling without stirring to 240 degrees F. on a candy thermometer, soft-ball stage. Remove from heat and beat with a wooden spoon until mixture begins to thicken. Beat in nuts and vanilla and pour into greased 9-inch square pan to cool. Cut into squares with a sharp knife when almost completely cooled. *Yield:* approximately 2½ dozen.

POPCORN BALLS

2 cups sugar
1½ cups water
½ cup white corn syrup
⅓ teaspoon salt
⅓ teaspoon vinegar
1 tablespoon vanilla
3 quarts popcorn, unsalted

Boil sugar, water, and corn syrup to 260 degrees F. on a candy thermometer. Add salt, vinegar, and vanilla and pour over popcorn in a large bowl. Mix syrup over all the popcorn and form into balls immediately. Place balls on large sheet of waxed paper to cool completely. *Yield:* approximately 12 balls.

BUTTER TAFFY

¾ cup butter or margarine
2 cups sugar
1 cup water

Melt butter or margarine in a saucepan. Add sugar and water. Bring to a boil and continue boiling to 290 degrees F. on a candy thermometer, crack stage. Pour into a greased 9-inch by 9-inch pan. When it begins to harden, cut into squares. *Yield:* approximately 25.

CHAPTER 17

JELLIES AND JAMS

Allergy Key: The recipes in this chapter are particularly for those who are allergic to the corn sugars or additives present in commercial jams and jellies. However, they can be used and enjoyed by anyone.

JELLIES

APPLE JELLY

> *2 pounds tart apples, cored and sliced but not*
> * peeled*
> *Water to cover apples*
> *Sugar*
> *Dampened jelly bag or cheesecloth bag*
> *Paraffin melted*

Put apples and water into a heavy saucepan and cook until apples are mushy. Strain, without pressing, through jelly bag or cheesecloth. If you squeeze the bag, the jelly will not be clear. Put juice back into pan; bring to a boil and add ¾ cup of sugar for each cup of juice. Cook over high heat until jelly first forms a sheet when dropped from a spoon. Stir with wooden spoon during cooking. Skim off the scum that rises to the top. Pour into sterilized glasses; cool and cover with a thin coat of melted paraffin. When this hardens, cover with a second thin coat. *Yield:* approximately 2 eight-ounce jelly glasses.

QUINCE JELLY

  2 pounds quinces, peeled and sliced
  Water to cover quinces
  Sugar
  Dampened jelly bag or cheesecloth
  Paraffin, melted

Proceed as in Apple Jelly*. *Yield:* approximately 2 eight-ounce jelly glasses.

RED CURRANT JELLY—COOKED

  2 pounds red currants
  1 pound white currants
  ½ pound red raspberries
  1 cup water
  Sugar
  Dampened jelly bag or cheesecloth
  Paraffin, melted

Wash the fruit and put it in a heavy saucepan with the water. Cook on a low fire for about 12 minutes. Then proceed as for Apple Jelly*. *Yield:* approximately 3 eight-ounce jelly glasses.

RED CURRANT JELLY—COLD PREPARATION

  2 pounds red currants
  1 pound white currants
  ½ pound red raspberries
  1 cup water
  1 pound confectioners' sugar
  Dampened jelly bag or cheesecloth
  Paraffin, melted

Wash the fruit and put it in a heavy saucepan with the water. Cook on a low fire for about 12 minutes. Add confectioners' sugar. Store in a cool place for about 4 hours, stirring often with a metal spoon until the sugar is dissolved. Fill the glasses and seal with 2 coats of paraffin as in Apple Jelly*. Refrigerate. This jelly is delicious, but very fragile and should not be kept longer than a month. *Yield:* approximately 3 eight-ounce jelly glasses.

TOMATO JELLY

> 10 pounds ripe tomatoes, peeled
> 2½ cups sugar
> 2 cups Apple Jelly*
> ½ stick vanilla
> Paraffin, melted

Put tomatoes through a meat grinder or food mill, then strain. Discard the pulp and seeds. Put tomato juice, sugar, Apple Jelly, and vanilla into a heavy saucepan and cook as for Apple Jelly*. Discard the vanilla before pouring into glasses. *Yield:* approximately 5 eight-ounce jelly glasses.

JAMS

APRICOT JAM

> 2 pounds ripe apricots
> 3 cups sugar
> ½ cup water
> Paraffin, melted

Cut apricots in half and remove pits. Crack pits and remove nut from inside; cut the nut into small pieces and set aside.

Put sugar and water in a heavy saucepan and cook for 5 minutes. Add apricots and cook over a moderate fire, stirring with a wooden spoon to prevent burning. Skim off the scum that rises to the top. Cook until jam just thickens. Add the chopped nut pieces, and pour into sterilized glasses. Cool completely and cover with 2 thin layers of paraffin as in Apple Jelly*. *Yield:* approximately 2 eight-ounce jelly glasses.

PLUM JAM

2 pounds stoned ripe plums, discard stones
3 cups sugar
½ cup water
Paraffin, melted

Proceed as for Apricot Jam*, except that if green gage plums are used, cook over a hot fire to preserve the color. *Yield:* approximately 2 eight-ounce jelly glasses.

RHUBARB JAM

3½ cups sugar
½ cup water
2 pounds rhubarb, peeled and cut into 1-inch
*   lengths (strawberry rhubarb is a good type)*
Paraffin, melted

Dissolve sugar in water and cook in a heavy saucepan for 10 minutes. Remove from fire and add rhubarb. Let stand for 10 minutes. Return to a hot fire and cook until jam just becomes thick. Skim off scum that rises to the top. Fill glasses as in Apple Jelly*. *Yield:* approximately 3 eight-ounce jelly glasses.

STRAWBERRY JAM

3 cups sugar
½ cup water
3 pints strawberries, cleaned and well drained
Paraffin, melted

Put sugar and water in a heavy saucepan and cook to 222 degrees F. on a candy thermometer. Add strawberries and remove from fire for about 10 minutes. Return to a hot fire and cook for 10 minutes. Remove strawberries from syrup; cook syrup again until it reaches 222 degrees F.; return strawberries to the syrup and cook again until jam just becomes thick. Throughout this process, keep skimming the scum that rises to the top. Place in sterilized glasses as in Apple Jelly*. *Yield:* approximately 4 eight-ounce jelly glasses.

TOMATO JAM

10 pounds ripe tomatoes, peeled
Dampened jelly bag or cheesecloth
4 cups sugar
¾ cup water
½ stick vanilla
1 cup red currant juice
Paraffin, melted

Put tomatoes through a meat grinder or strainer. Cook for 10 minutes over a medium heat. Filter through jelly bag or cheesecloth, discarding the liquid and keeping the pulp.

Place sugar, water, and vanilla in a heavy saucepan and cook to 215 degrees F. on a candy thermometer. Add tomato pulp and currant juice. Cook over a hot fire, stirring with a wooden spoon and skimming off the scum that rises to the top. Cook until jam just becomes thick. Discard vanilla. Place in sterilized glasses as in Apple Jelly*. *Yield:* approximately 5 eight-ounce jelly glasses.

CHAPTER 18

SYRUPS

Allergy Key: Since many people are allergic to corn sugars, synthetic additives and preservatives, and other ingredients found in commercial syrups, we have prepared this chapter. You may select the proper syrup for your purpose on the basis of flavor, color, and allergy.

Uses: Syrups can be used as cold drinks by adding cold water to desired consistency, or as carbonated drinks by adding soda water. When thickened as described at the end of this chapter, they can be used over ice cream to make sundaes, or on puddings, cakes, fresh fruit, or whatever desired.

The simple syrups can be kept for 2 weeks. The rest should be used within a few days. All should be kept refrigerated.

SIMPLE SYRUPS

HEAT PROCESS:

> *3 pounds (6 cups) sugar*
> *1 quart water*

Mix the ingredients in a saucepan. Bring to a boil, strain and store in a glass container. *Yield:* approximately 3⅔ cups.

COLD PROCESS:

   3 *pounds (6 cups) sugar*
   1 *quart cold water*

Place in glass container and stir with wooden paddle until sugar is dissolved. *Yield:* approximately 3⅔ cups.

ROCK CANDY SYRUP

   2 *pounds rock candy*
   2 *cups water*

Place ingredients in a saucepan and bring to a boil. Reduce heat and simmer in pan until candy is dissolved. Strain and store in glass container. *Yield:* approximately 3½ cups.

COMPLEX SYRUPS

ALMOND SYRUP

   ¼ *pound sweet unblanched almonds*
   2 *ounces bitter almonds*
   1 *quart water*
   1 *pound (2 cups) sugar*
   1 *teaspoon orange extract*

Crush almonds. Add water and simmer for 20 minutes. Add sugar and stir until it dissolves. Strain. When cool, add orange extract. Store in a glass container. *Yield:* approximately 1½ quarts.

CHOCOLATE SYRUP

1½ pounds (3 cups) sugar
¾ cup cocoa
1 quart water

Mix sugar, cocoa, and water. Bring to a boil. Cool and store in a glass container. *Yield:* approximately 1½ quarts.

CITRUS FRUIT SYRUP

3 lemons or 3 oranges or 2 grapefruits
1 pound (2 cups) sugar
1 quart water

Grate rind of fruit. Mix with sugar and set aside for 4 hours. Then combine all ingredients. Bring to a boil and strain. Cool and store in glass container. *Yield:* approximately 1½ quarts.

CLARET SYRUP

1 quart dry claret
1 quart Simple Syrup*
⅛ cup orange or lemon juice

Mix ingredients and serve immediately. *Yield:* approximately 2 quarts.

CLOVE SYRUP

⅜ cup crushed cloves
2 cups hot water
2 quarts Simple Syrup*

Steep the cloves in the hot water for 30 minutes. Strain; add syrup and store in a glass container. *Yield:* 2½ quarts.

COFFEE SYRUP

1 cup plus 1½ teaspoons finely ground fresh coffee
1½ quarts water
3 pounds (6 cups) sugar

Mix coffee with 2 cups cold water, and let steep for 2 hours. Add remaining water and sugar. Bring to a boil. Strain and store in a glass container. *Yield:* approximately 2 quarts.

CREAM SYRUP

2 cups condensed milk or non-dairy milk substitute
2 cups water
3 cups sugar

Combine ingredients and heat to boiling point. Strain and store in a glass container. *Yield:* approximately 1¼ quarts.

CREAM NECTAR SYRUP

1 pint 36 per cent cream (whipping cream) or
non-dairy whipping cream substitute
1 cup Orange Syrup (see Citrus Fruit Syrup*)

1 cup Pineapple Syrup (see Fruit Juice Syrup*)
1 cup sugar
4 drops vanilla extract

Combine first four ingredients and heat to boiling point. Strain. When cool, add vanilla extract. Store in a glass container. *Yield:* approximately 1 quart.

FRUIT JUICE SYRUP

2 cups fruit juice, from any of the following fruits: strawberry—raspberry—blackberry—blueberry—cranberry—apple—peach—apricot—pineapple—fruit should be fresh and ripe
2 cups Simple Syrup*
1 tablespoon lemon juice

Bring juice and syrup to just below the boiling point. Strain; cool; add lemon juice and store in glass container. *Yield:* approximately 1 quart.

HONEY MINT SYRUP

½ cup crushed and minced mint leaves
¼ cup sugar
1 cup hot water
2 cups honey
2 quarts Simple Syrup*

Combine mint, sugar, and water. Bring to a boil. Steep for 1 hour; strain; add honey and Simple Syrup. Store in a glass container. *Yield:* approximately 2½ quarts.

TEA SYRUP

   1⅝ cups orange pekoe tea leaves
   1 quart water
   1 quart Rock Candy Syrup*

Bring tea and water to a boil. Let steep for 30 minutes. Strain; add syrup and store in a glass container. *Yield:* approximately 2 quarts.

TO THICKEN SYRUPS:

   1 tablespoon arrowroot starch, cornstarch, or potato
      starch
   ¼ *cup cold water*

Dissolve starch in the cold water. Add to the syrup and bring to a boil, stirring constantly.

APPENDIX

This Appendix contains special indexes to aid in selecting recipes for the most common allergies. Only those chapters which present difficult recipe selection problems are included in the index. Each index contains a list of the chapters included in it.

CORN-FREE INDEX

* Use baking powder without cornstarch.

* Use baking powder without cornstarch.

* Use baking powder without cornstarch.

EGG-FREE INDEX

MILK-FREE INDEX

** Uses milk substitute.

WHEAT-FREE INDEX

Corn Muffins *153*
Cornstarch Puff Paste *185*
Cranberry Pie *182*

Eggdrop for Soup *69*
Egg-Free No-Chocolate Chocolate Cake *160*

Fresh Fruit Pie *182*

Gingerbread Men *170*

Ice Cream Muffins *154*

Jelly Roll *166*

Lady Baltimore Cake *162*
Lord Baltimore Cake *163*

Maple Icing *188*
Mashed Potato and Rye Muffins *154*
Meringue Cookies *171*
Mincemeat Pie *181*

No-Chocolate Chocolate Brownies *178*
No-Chocolate Chocolate Cake—I *158*
No-Chocolate Chocolate Cake—II *159*
No-Chocolate Chocolate Cake—III *160*
No-Chocolate Reese Roll *164*
Noodles for Soup or Spaghetti—I *69*

Noodles for Soup or Spaghetti—III *70*
Nut Balls *173*
Nut Meringue Cookies *173*

Oatmeal Bars *178*
Oatmeal Cookies *174*
Orange Roll *164*
Orange Sauce Icing *189*

Pastry *184*
Peanut Butter Cookies—I *174*
Peanut Butter Cookies—II *175*
Pie Shell *179*
Potato Starch Muffins *154*
Potato Starch Sponge Cake *166*
Pumpkin Pie—I *183*
Pumpkin Pie—II *183*
Pure Rye Bread *148*

Rice and Rye Flour Muffins *155*
Rice Flour and Potato Starch Muffins *156*
Rice Flour Jelly Roll *167*
Rice Flour Muffins *155*
Rice Flour Pie Crust *180*
Rice Flour Sponge Cake *167*
Rice or Barley Cookies *175*
Rye and Barley Bread *149*
Rye and Potato Bread *150*

Sweet Potato Pie *184*

White Icing *188*

EGG- AND CORN-FREE INDEX

Applesauce Cake *162*
Apricot Water Ice *191*

Barley and Potato Bread *150*
Barley Flour Pie Crust *179*
*Barley Muffins *152*
Butterscotch Icing *187*
Butterscotch Shortbread *176*
Butter Taffy *203*

Candied Grapefruit Peel *201*
Candied Orange Peel *200*
Cantaloupe Ice *194*
Cherry Water Ice *190*
Cinnamon Butter Cookies *168*
Coconut Cream Candy *199*
Coconut Crust *180*
Currant Ice *190*

Egg-Free No-Chocolate Chocolate
  Cake *160*

Fresh Fruit Pie *182*

Grape Water Ice *191*

Honeydew Ice *195*

*Ice Cream Muffins *154*

Lemon Sherbet *195*
Lemon Water Ice *192*
Lime Water Ice *192*

Maple Icing *188*
*Mashed Potato and Rye Muf-
  fins *154*
Mincemeat Pie *181*
Mints *201*

Nectarine Water Ice *193*
No-Chocolate Chocolate Fudge
  200

Orange Sauce Icing *189*
Orange Sherbet *195*

Peach Water Ice *193*
Peanut Butter Fudge *201*
Penuche *202*
Pie Shell *179*
Pure Rye Bread *148*

Raspberry Water Ice *194*
*Rice and Rye Flour Muffins
  155
*Rice Flour Muffins *155*
Rice Flour Pie Crust *180*
*Rice or Barley Cookies *175*
Rye and Barley Bread *149*
Rye and Potato Bread *150*

Scotch Shortbread *176*

Watermelon Ice *194*
White Bread *151*

* Use baking powder without cornstarch.

MILK- AND CORN-FREE INDEX

* Use baking powder without cornstarch.
** Uses milk substitute.

* Use baking powder without cornstarch.
** Uses milk substitute.

MILK- AND EGG-FREE INDEX

** Uses milk substitute.

** Uses milk substitute.

EGG- AND WHEAT-FREE INDEX

MILK- AND WHEAT-FREE INDEX

** Uses milk substitute.

** Uses milk substitute.

MILK-, EGG-, AND CORN-FREE INDEX

* Use baking powder without cornstarch.

* Use baking powder without cornstarch.
** Uses milk substitute.

MILK-, WHEAT-, AND EGG-FREE INDEX

** Uses milk substitute.

MILK-, WHEAT-, EGG-, AND CORN-FREE INDEX

* Use baking powder without cornstarch.
** Uses milk substitute.

*Rice and Rye Flour Muffins
155
*Rice Flour Muffins   155
Rice Flour Pie Crust   180

*Rice or Barley Cookies   175
Rye and Barley Bread   149
Rye and Potato Bread   150

* Use baking powder without cornstarch.

RYE-FREE INDEX

NO-CHOCOLATE CHOCOLATE INDEX

INDEX

Bean Salad, Navy, 41
Bean Soup, Marrow, 30
Bean Sprouts, Creamed, 59
Béarnaise Sauce, 89–90
Beaulieu Salad, 39
Beef, 120–24
    Borsch with, 25–26
    Brisket, Braised Fresh, 120–21
    Cooking Methods, 117–20
    Flemish Carbonades, 121
    Goulash, Hungarian, 123
    Hamburgers, Tiny, 21
    Liver Vizcaya, 133–34
    Meat Balls with, 132
    Meat Loaf with, 132
    Parisian, 15
    Pickling, 137
    Pot Roast of, 124
    Rolls, Dried, 15
    Shish Kabob, 122–23
    Short Ribs, 122
    Stock, 24
    Tenderloin, Roast, 120
    Tenderloin Teriyaki, 22
    Tongue (see Tongue)
Beer, 3
    Soup, 25
Beets, Cooking Methods, 56–57
    Vinaigrette, 43
Beet Salad, 39
Beet Soup, Borsch, 25–26
Beet Sugar, 12
Benedictine, 4
Bisque, Lobster, 36
Bisque, Shrimp, 35
Blinis and Caviar, 19–20
Bluefish, Boiled, 106
Bluefish, Broiled, 106
Bluefish, Pan Fried, 108
Bordelaise Sauce, 90
Borsch, 25–26
    German, 26
Bouillabaisse, 109
Brabançonne Salad, 39–40
Brandy, 3
Breads, 148–56
    Barley Muffins, 152–53
        Potato and, 150–51
        Rye and, 149
    Corn, 152
    Corn Muffins, 153
        Potato Starch and, 153
    Ice Cream Muffins, 154

Potato and Barley, 150–51
Potato and Rye, 150
    Muffins, 154–55
Potato Starch Muffins, 154–55
    Cornmeal and, 153
    Rice Flour and, 156
Rice Flour Muffins, 155
    Potato Starch and, 156
    Rye Flour and, 155
Rye, 148–49
    Barley and, 149
    Potato and, 150
    Potato and Rye Muffins, 154–55
    Rice Flour and Rye Muffins, 155
    Sourdough, 152
White, 151
Yeast-Free, 151–56
Brine, Pickling, for Meats, 136–37
Broccoli, Cooking Methods, 56–57
    Milanese, 57
    Vinaigrette, 43
Brownies, Butterscotch, 177
    No-Chocolate Chocolate, 178
Brown Sauce with Starch, 87–88
Brown Sauce with Wheat Flour, 87
Brown Sugar, 12
    Meringue Cookies, 172
Brussels Sprouts, Cooking Methods, 56–57
Burnt Almond Maple Mousse, 196
Butter, 13
    Cookies, 168
        Cinnamon, 168–69
    Sauce, 90
    Taffy, 203
Butterscotch Brownies, 177
Butterscotch Icing, 187
Butterscotch Shortbread, 176

Cabbage, Cooking Methods, 56–58
    Salad, Red, 40
Cakes, 158–67
    Angel Food, 161
    Applesauce, 162
    Jelly Roll, 166–67
        Rice Flour, 167
    Lady Baltimore, 162–63
    Lord Baltimore, 163
    No-Chocolate Chocolate, 58–61
        Egg-Free, 160–61
    No-Chocolate Reese Roll, 164–65
    Orange Roll, 164
    Potato Starch Sponge, 166

*Chocolate bars
2 cups Rice Krispies
4 tblsps margarine
6 oz choc chips
1/4 cup corn syrup
1 1/2 cups sugar*

75 76 77 10 9 8 7 6 5 4 3 2 1